The

THE MOMENTOUS EVENT

*A discussion of scripture teaching
on the second advent*

W. J. GRIER

THE BANNER OF TRUTH TRUST

THE BANNER OF TRUTH TRUST
3 Murrayfield Road, Edinburgh EH12 6EL
PO Box 621, Carlisle, PA 17013, USA

*

© W. J. Grier 1945
First published by the Evangelical Bookshop, Belfast, 1945
Reprinted 1946, 1952, 1959, 1963
First Banner of Truth edition, 1970
Reprinted 1976
Reprinted 1986
Reprinted 1997
Reprinted 2006
Reprinted 2013

ISBN: 978 0 85151 020 0

*

Printed in the USA by
Versa Press Inc.,
East Peoria, IL

Author's foreword

THE chapters of this book were originally written as articles for *The Irish Evangelical* (now *The Evangelical Presbyterian*), a monthly which I have edited for over forty years. They appeared in the issues from March 1944 to June 1945. After their appearance in this way, a close friend urged that they be made available in book form. So it came about that in December 1945 the first edition of this volume appeared.

I am indebted to my one-time fellow-student and life-long friend, the late Professor N. B. Stonehouse, for helpful suggestions at a few points in chapter 15. Acknowledgments to others have been made in the text. If in any case due acknowledgment has been overlooked, I am sincerely sorry.

This little book has enjoyed a circulation beyond all my hopes. A fresh printing – the sixth – has been undertaken by the Banner of Truth Trust, to whose ministry so many are indebted. It is sent forth in this new format with the prayer that it may serve to kindle expectation and longing for 'the momentous event' itself and for the grace to be brought to His own at His appearing (1 Peter 1:13).

TO MY WIFE

Contents

	Author's Foreword	5
1.	*The Momentous Event*	9
2.	*'Post,' 'Pre,' or 'Non'*	13
3.	*The Fathers and the Millennium*	19
4.	*The Reformers and the Millennium*	29
5.	*The Interpretation of Old Testament Prophecy*	33
6.	*The New Testament Interpretation of Old Testament Prophecy*	43
7.	*Some General Considerations from the New Testament*	53
8.	*Christ's Teaching as to His Second Coming*	61
9.	*The Second Coming in Early Apostolic Preaching*	67
10.	*The Victory over Death*	73
11.	*New Heavens and a New Earth*	79
12.	*Three Views of Revelation*	87
13.	*The Witness of Revelation*	95
14.	*The Pre-Millennial View of Revelation* 20	103
15.	*Satan, a Defeated and Doomed Foe*	109
16.	*Is the Momentous Event Near?*	121
	Epilogue	125
	Appendix: *The Seventy Weeks of Daniel* 9	127

Surely I come quickly

REV. 22:20

Surely He cometh, and a thousand voices
  Shout to the saints and to the deaf are dumb;
Surely He cometh, and the earth rejoices,
  Glad in His coming, Who hath sworn, I come.

FROM F. W. H. MYERS' ST PAUL

1 : *The momentous event*

THE great event of the future is the second advent of our Lord Jesus Christ. The Scriptures plainly declare that this advent will be personal, visible, sudden and unexpected, glorious and triumphant.

Personal

The New Testament teaches that our Lord will come in person. While the Scriptures refer to great events in the history of the individual, like death, and great events in the history of the Church, like the outpouring of the Spirit at Pentecost and the destruction of Jerusalem, as comings of Christ, yet they also declare in no uncertain language that there is to be a final triumphant return of Christ towering far above these other partial and typical comings. 'The Lord *himself* shall descend from heaven' (1 Thess. 4:16).

Visible

It is clearly taught in the New Testament that the Lord will return visibly. His first coming was literal and visible, and we may be sure that His second coming, which is so often linked with it in Scripture statements, will be literal and visible too. 'This same Jesus, which is taken up from you into heaven, shall so come in like manner as ye have seen him go into heaven' (Acts 1:11); His second coming is to be as visible as His ascension. 'Then shall appear the sign of the Son of man in heaven: and then shall all the tribes of the earth mourn, and *they shall see* the Son of man coming in the clouds of heaven with power and great glory. And he shall send his angels with a great sound of a trumpet, and they shall gather together his elect from the four winds, from one end of heaven to the other' (Matt. 24:30, 31).

The late Dr R. V. Bingham once held the common doctrine of a secret appearing of the Lord and a secret rapture of the saints, but, on being asked by his wife for a proof-text, he found that he could not produce one. There are plenty of texts on the other side. Surely if it were to be secret, it would not be 'with a shout, with the voice of the archangel, and with the trump of God' (1 Thess. 4:16).

Sudden and Unexpected

Speaking about the word 'apocalypse,' or 'revelation,' of the Lord, used in the New Testament for His second coming, Dr Geerhardus Vos says that the 'very idea of suddenness and unexpectedness seems to be intimately associated with the word.' (*Pauline Eschatology*, p. 79). It is as if a curtain were suddenly flung aside and the Lord of glory revealed. His coming will be 'as a thief in the night. For when they shall say, Peace and safety; then sudden destruction cometh upon them' (1 Thess. 5:2, 3). The Saviour Himself said that His coming would be 'as the lightning' (Matt. 24:27) – as sudden, and as universally visible. None will foresee it and all will see it at once. What a warning this should be to careless sinners and to slack, easy-going professors of religion!

Glorious and Triumphant

The contrast is often drawn in the New Testament between the two appearings of our Lord. He came in the body of His humiliation, but He will come in the body of His glory (Heb. 9:28). He 'took the form of a servant,' but when He comes again 'every knee shall bow' to Him (Phil. 2:5–11). He came to be rejected and killed, but He will come 'in his own glory and the glory of his Father and of the holy angels' (Luke 9:22–26). He came as a child but He will come as King of kings and Lord of lords, victorious over every foe (Rev. 12:5; 19:11–16).

One of the common New Testament words for Christ's 'coming' would be more properly translated 'arrival.' The New Testament writers recognised indeed that Christ had already arrived, but *'the arrival,'* the epochal coming, the one fully worthy of the name, belonged to the future. They had an intensively prospective outlook – for them the momentous event is the coming of the Lord.

Another word for His second coming – 'the revelation' – is used in the same way, as if this, rather than His first coming, was *the revelation* par excellence.

Another term for it is 'the day' – 'the night is far spent, the day is at hand' (Rom. 13:12). When He comes, darkness will vanish for ever for His own, and deliverance, joy, and blessedness will be ushered in. Indeed, His second advent is described as 'our redemption.'

J. A. Bengel says beautifully (on Acts 1:11) – 'Between His ascension and His coming no event intervenes equal in importance to these: therefore, these two are joined together. Naturally, then, the apostles . . . set before them the day of Christ as very near. And it accords with the majesty of Christ that during the whole period between

11

His ascension and His advent, He should without intermission be expected.'

It was characteristic of the saints of the Old Testament that they looked for the consolation of Israel, Christ's first coming. *Now* 'this is pinned as a badge to the sleeve of every true believer, that he looketh for and longeth for Christ's (second) coming' (John Trapp). The New Testament keeps this great event constantly before our minds and urges it on our attention, that we may be active, earnest, patient, joyful, and holy.

2 : '*Post*,' '*pre*,' or '*non*'

Post-Millennialism

Post-MILLENNIALISM teaches that the second coming of Christ will follow the millennium. The kingdom of Christ is now in existence and will gradually extend its borders through the preaching of the gospel. At the close of the gospel dispensation there will be a millennial period when Christianity will prevail upon the earth. Evil, which will make progress alongside of good up to the millennium, will during the millennium be restrained, and Satan will be bound. The millennium will be followed by an outbreak of wickedness and a terrible final conflict with the forces of evil led by Satan, and there will ensue simultaneously Christ's second coming, the resurrection of all the dead, and the final judgment.

It may be objected to this view, and we feel there is some force in the objection, that the Bible does not hold forth the prospect of a converted world before the Lord comes; are not the wheat and the tares to grow together till the harvest at the end of the world? Moreover, it does not quite seem to harmonise with the idea of a millennium of prevailing righteousness that, at its close, Satan will be found leading a host to battle from the four quarters of the earth, whose number is as the sand of the sea (Rev. 20:8). Where are they to come from, if righteousness prevails in a converted world (Cp. Luke 18:8; II Thess. 2:1-12)?

Pre-Millennialism

Pre-millennialism holds that Christ's second coming will not follow, but will introduce the millennium. The order of events, according to the common pre-millennial view, is as follows:

(1) A period of apostasy preceding the Lord's coming.

(2) The Lord will come in secret, and will raise the dead saints, snatching them away together with the living believers – an event commonly called the 'secret rapture.'

(3) There will ensue a short seven-year period of great tribulation, in which the Antichrist will rule the earth.

(4) Then Christ will appear from heaven openly, Armageddon will be fought and Christ will overthrow Antichrist and the hosts of evil. This will usher in the Redeemer's glorious reign at Jerusalem, and the temple and the sacrificial worship will be restored.

(5) At the end of the thousand years, Satan will be loosed again, and will stir up rebellion against God. His crushing defeat will be followed by the resurrection of the wicked and their judgment and the eternal state.

There are pre-millennialists who do not accept the above scheme. They do not believe in a secret rapture, and they do believe that the Church will pass through the tribulation and will be on earth during the rise and reign of Antichrist. This pre-millennial view, therefore, rejects the idea of a two-stage coming of Christ before the millennium, and holds that Christ will appear openly to take away His saints and to overthrow Antichrist and establish His millennial kingdom on earth. This view can claim to be the older pre-millennial view, as it is similar to the millennial views held by some fathers in the early Church.

Many pre-millennialists hold that Christ intended to establish the kingdom of His father David when He was

on earth – a national kingdom. Because the Jews refused
to repent, this kingdom was postponed till His second
coming, when it will be set up, and He will reign at
Jerusalem. This view is open to very serious objection
indeed. It tends to challenge Job's affirmation, 'No purpose
of Thine can be restrained.' It supposes that Jesus made a
national offer of an earthly kingdom to the Jews, whereas
He made no such offer; indeed, when they would have
made Him a king, He would not have it (John 6:15).
Moreover, it makes the kingdom an earthly and national
institution, while the New Testament preaches entirely a
spiritual and eternal kingdom from every nation and tribe
and tongue. It also fails to explain how glorified saints and
people still in the flesh can live and associate together
during the thousand years. Instead of 'people still in the
flesh,' we might have said 'sinners in the flesh,' for though
righteousness is supposed to prevail in the millennium, yet
at its close Satan is to lead a host to battle from the four
quarters of the earth whose number is as the sand of the
sea (Rev. 20:8)! Lastly, as Louis Berkhof states, this
pre-millennial view 'erroneously seeks its main support in
a passage (Rev. 20:1–6) which represents a scene in heaven
and makes no mention whatever of the Jews, of an earthly
and national kingdom, nor of the land of Palestine.'

The common New Testament teaching does not give us
two, three, or even four resurrections. The New Testament
speaks again and again of the resurrection of just and unjust in one breath. It speaks of the Lord's coming bringing
blessing to His own, and at the very same time 'destruction' to the ungodly. The Saviour Himself taught the
resurrection of His people at 'the last day' (John 6:39, 40,
44, 54; John 11:24), at the very same 'last day' on which
judgment will come upon the wicked (John 12:48).

15

Non-Millennialism

The non-millennialist believes that 'post' and 'pre' have erred in interpreting Revelation 20 as teaching a thousand years of *earthly* blessedness, and, in particular, that the latter has erred in forecasting an age whose joys are shared by thousands of Christ-rejecting men who survive the tribulation and the advent. Some post-millennialists, like B. B. Warfield, agree with the non-millennial view of Revelation 20, but on the basis of other Scriptures look for a 'golden age' before Christ comes.

The non-millennialist sees no ground in Scripture for a millennium before the Lord's coming, and he holds that the possibility of a millennium after His coming is excluded by New Testament teaching.

He agrees with the 'pre' view that the world will not be converted before the Lord's coming by the preaching of the gospel; while he agrees with the 'post' view that the second coming ushers in the end of the world, the last judgment, and the eternal state.

The order of events, according to the non-millenarian, is as follows:

(1) The second coming will be preceded by widespread apostasy from the true faith, which will come to a climax in the appearance of Antichrist.

(2) This final rebellion against Christ will be overthrown by Him at His personal appearing, when He will come from heaven to take to Himself His own people, believers who have died being raised and living believers being changed.

(3) At this coming, the wicked dead will also be raised for judgment. The earth and the works that are therein will be overwhelmed in fire (2 Pet. 3), and a new heaven and new earth will appear, in which only righteousness dwells.

All three of these views have been held by saintly men. The non-millenarian view has been held from early times (see Berkhof's *Systematic Theology*, p. 708) and by N. B. Stonehouse and William Hendriksen in our day; the post-millenarian has been widely held by orthodox divines, among others by John Bunyan and B. B. Warfield; and the pre-millenarian, while it never became so widely held as to secure a place in the great creeds of the Church, can claim devoted men like Andrew Bonar among its adherents.

3: *The fathers and the millennium*

D R CHARLES FEINBERG, one of the latest advocates of the pre-millennial view, asserts it as an admitted fact that 'the entire early Church of the first three centuries was pre-millennial, almost to a man'. (*Pre-millennialism or A-millennialism*, pp. 27, 202). The writings of the early Church have been translated, and the ordinary English reader can turn to them and see for himself if this be so. It should be of interest to us to know what the men close to the apostles, in the days of the Church's primitive purity, taught – men such as Clement of Rome, who is taken by some (without solid grounds) to be the associate and fellow-labourer of the apostle Paul, mentioned in Philippians 4:3, and Polycarp of Smyrna, a disciple of the apostle John, who claimed to have been familiar with those who saw the Lord.

The Apostolic Fathers

The First Epistle of Clement is sometimes dated as early as A.D. 90 and sometimes as late as A.D. 97. It stood in very high esteem in ancient times, and deservedly so. Clement mentions the coming again of Christ and a future resurrection, but has no hint of two resurrections or of a resurrection of the righteous only or of a millennial kingdom on earth.

The so-called *Second Epistle of Clement* was probably

written between A.D. 120–140. It looks forward to Christ's second coming, the resurrection, the judgment, and the life everlasting, but says not a word of any millennial kingdom on earth. The kingdom to which it looks is not a thing of earth and time; in it the promises are fully realised, things which eye hath not seen, nor ear heard, neither have entered into the heart of man.

Polycarp writes (about A.D. 110) of Christ as follows: 'To Him all things in heaven and earth are subject. Him every spirit serves. He comes as the Judge of the living and the dead. His blood will God require of those who do not believe in Him. But He Who raised Him from the dead will raise us up also.' Polycarp seems to look for a general judgment at Christ's second coming. He certainly has not a word of a millennial kingdom on earth.

Ignatius, from whose pen we have quite a number of letters, written as he was on his way to die in the arena at Rome, is taken up with the glorious prospect of a martyr's death. He writes 'These are the last times.' But of events at the end he says nothing whatever. At any rate, Dr Feinberg cannot claim him.

The Didache, or *Teaching of the Twelve Apostles*, is a Church manual which was drawn up very early in the second century. Here is what the sixteenth chapter of the *Didache* has to say about the end of the world:

'Watch over your life; let not your lamps be quenched and let not your loins be unloosed, but be ye ready; for ye know not the hour in which our Lord cometh. . . . In the last days the false prophets and destroyers shall be multiplied, . . . for when lawlessness increases, they shall hate and persecute and deliver one another up; and then shall appear the world-deceiver as Son of God, and shall do signs and wonders, and the earth shall be delivered into

his hands, and he shall commit iniquities which
yet come to pass from the beginning of the wor

'And then shall the race of men come into the
trial, and many shall be offended and shall perish; but
who endure in their faith shall be saved under the cur
itself.

'And then shall appear the sign of the truth: first the
sign of the opening in heaven; then the voice of the trumpet; and third, the resurrection of the dead. Not, however,
of all, but as was said: "The Lord shall come and all His
saints with Him." Then shall the world see the Lord
coming upon the clouds of heaven.'

This passage teaches the coming of a personal Antichrist
whom it calls 'the world-deceiver'. The tribulation under
him is not for Jews or 'tribulation saints' only, as commonly held by pre-millenarians, but for the whole 'race
of men'; and there is certainly no trace of a 'secret rapture'
before it begins.

It is urged, however, that there is a distinction between
the resurrection of saints and that of sinners, and pre-
millenarians are quick to insert their thousand years
between the two. They have missed the point. The point
is that the resurrection of saints is the final sign preceding
the Lord's coming. To this form of expression others than
pre-millenarians can consent. Geerhardus Vos, a non-
millenarian, in his book on *Pauline Eschatology*, says (on
1 Cor. 15:23, 24) that 'a brief interval in logical conception
at least must be assumed' between the resurrection of
believers and 'the end'; but Dr Vos goes on immediately
to insist that this by no means opens the door to a rounded-
off period of a thousand years.

The *Didache* has no reference to an earthly millennium.
If the writer had believed in one, he would most likely

pre-millenarian who could
; an important part of his
t.

from the first half of the
aled to as pre-millenarian.
ot look in that direction:
thout respect of persons.
... has done: if he is righteous, his
g...ousness will precede him; if he is wicked, the reward
of wickedness is before him.' This looks like a general
judgment. So does this: 'The day is at hand on which all
things shall perish with the Evil One. The Lord is near
and His reward.' He also urges his readers to inquire what
the Lord asks from them and to 'do it that ye may be safe
in the day of judgment.'

Barnabas' scheme of history was patterned on the week
of creation in Genesis 1. The expression 'He finished in
six days' means, he says, that 'the Lord will finish all
things in six thousand years.' The expression 'He rested
on the seventh day' contains the prophetic meaning that
when Christ, coming again, 'shall destroy the time of the
wicked man, and judge the ungodly, and change the sun
and the moon and the stars, then shall He truly rest on the
seventh day.'

Pre-millenarians take this seventh day of the millennium, but what pre-millenarian is willing to admit that the
millennium is ushered in by the judgment of the ungodly,
as Barnabas states? According to the Epistle of Barnabas,
the seventh day will not come till 'wickedness is no longer
existing, and all things have been made new.' The eighth
day is 'the beginning of another world', but all distinction
seems to be done away between the seventh and eighth
day, when Barnabas says that the Lord, in giving rest to

all things (which happens on the seventh day) 'makes the beginning of the eighth day, that is, the beginning of another world.'

It is clear, at any rate, that Barnabas shuts out the possibility of an earthly millennium in which unregenerate men will be under the reign of Christ. It is perfectly clear too that he holds, as all others of his time, that Christians and not Jews are the heirs of the covenant. It is interesting to note that D. H. Kromminga, a pre-millenarian, says the presumption is that 'Barnabas was what we nowadays call an a-millennialist' (*Millennium in the Church*, p. 33).

The beautiful little *Epistle to Diognetus* speaks of a future kingdom, but it is in heaven, and will be given to those who love Christ.

In his Ecclesiastical History, Eusebius, the learned historian of the fourth century, tells of a tradition handed down by an ecclesiastical writer of distinguished rank, named *Hegesippus*. This tradition refers to two members 'of the family of our Lord, the grandchildren of Jude, the brother of our Lord.' They were reported as being of the family of David, and the rumour of the existence of members of this royal line alarmed the Emperor Domitian (A.D. 81–96). They were brought before him, and he asked if they were of David's race and what property and money they had. Though of David's line, they had only a piece of land of thirty-nine acres. They showed their horny hands as evidences of their toil. When asked about Christ's kingdom and when and where it would appear, they said 'that it was not a temporal or an earthly kingdom, but celestial and angelic; that it would appear at the end of the world, when, coming in glory, He would judge the quick and the dead, and give to every one according to his works.' These

23

two worthies of the close of the first century were certainly no believers in an earthly millennial kingdom.

In the first half of the second century there are really only two to whom we can point with any certainty as holding a future reign of Christ on earth for a thousand years – Papias and Justin Martyr. There was, of course, the heretic Cerinthus also.

To Irenæus and Eusebius we are indebted for some fragments from Papias. *Papias* pictures in extravagant language the ten thousand-fold fruitfulness of the earth during the millennium. Eusebius says that Papias passed on 'certain strange parables of our Lord and of His doctrine and some other matters rather too fabulous. In these he (Papias) says there would be a certain millennium after the resurrection, and that there would be a corporeal reign of Christ on this very earth; which things he appears to have imagined, as if they were authorised by the apostolic narrations, not understanding correctly, . . . for he is very limited in his comprehension, as is evident from his discourses.' Eusebius does not think highly of the premillenarian views of Papias, apparently. It was through Papias, according to Eusebius, that Irenæus and many others 'were carried away by a similar opinion.'

When *Justin Martyr* is speaking of the kingdom for which Christians look, he denies that it is a human kingdom – 'You suppose we speak of a human kingdom, whereas we speak of that which is with God.' Justin speaks of a general judgment at Christ's second coming, when death 'shall for ever quit those who believe on Him and be no more: when some are sent to be punished unceasingly into judgment and condemnation of fire; but others shall exist in freedom from suffering, from corruption, and from grief and in immortality.'

From these statements one would suppose there was no room for an earthly millennium in his teaching, yet inconsistently he says elsewhere that there will be a resurrection of the dead and a thousand years in Jerusalem, which will then be built, adorned, and enlarged, and 'that thereafter the general and, in short, the eternal resurrection and judgment of all men would likewise take place.' Justin's millennium would have no special place at all for the Jew, for he tells us over and over that Christians 'are the true Israelite race'. He tells us that he and others who are right-minded Christians on all points hold to this notion of a millennium, but he admits that 'many who belong to the pure and pious faith and are true Christians think otherwise.'

Papias and Justin, then, are the only two of all the writers in the first sixty years of the second century who may with any certainty be called pre-millenarians, and Justin is decidedly inconsistent. Others definitely by their statements exclude pre-millenarianism. The first two volumes of the Fathers in the Ante-Nicene Library contain 950 pages, but the indices give only two references under the word 'millennium'; these two are to the statements of Papias and Justin.

The Old Catholic Church

Let us pass from the Apostolic Fathers to the Old Catholic Church (A.D. 150–250). This period Dr Shedd calls 'the blooming age of millenarianism.' He holds, however, that even at this time 'it does not become the catholic faith, as embodied in the catholic creed.' The Apostles' Creed in its earlier forms comes to us from this time, and, according to it, there is no corporeal advent of Christ upon earth after His ascension on high, until He leaves His session with the Father and comes directly 'from thence' to the last Judgment.

Irenæus (about A.D. 180) taught an earthly millennium, but a millennium whose benefits were exclusively for the saved and in which the wicked and unregenerate have no part. Irenæus speaks of opposers of his millenarian views who held the catholic faith.

The Montanists, one of the wildest sects, flourished at the close of the second and the beginning of the third centuries. They preached the near approach of the millennial reign.

One of their leading prophetesses, Maximilla, said, 'After me there is no more prophecy, but only the end of the world'. The new Jerusalem was to come down in the village of Pepuza in Phrygia. They were the warmest premillenarians in the ancient Church, and through them that view spread widely.

Caius of Rome attacked the Montanists, and went so far as to ascribe pre-millenarianism in its origin to the heretic Cerinthus! *Hippolytus*, the most learned member of the Church at Rome in the beginning of the third century, also opposed the Montanists. He wrote a treatise on the Anti-Christ – 'How he shall stir up tribulation and persecution against the saints'. The Church will pass through the tribulation under Antichrist, according to Hippolytus, and 'the whole world finally approaching the consummation, what remains but the coming of our Lord and Saviour Jesus Christ from heaven, for whom we have looked in hope, who shall bring the conflagration and just judgment upon all who have refused to believe on Him.' When Christ comes, says Hippolytus, the earthly will be done away 'that the eternal and indestructible kingdom of the saints may appear'; when He comes He will destroy His enemies and give the eternal kingdom to His saints. In view of such language, Hippolytus cannot be reckoned a pre-millenarian.

The third century witnessed a very decided opposition to belief in an earthly millennium. Origen argued against it. His arguments at length gained a complete victory. Lactantius was the only man of note in the fourth century who still held the system. Athanasius, the great defender of the doctrine of the deity of Christ against the Arians, speaks of Christ coming to judge the world; the good will then receive the heavenly kingdom and the evil will be cast into the eternal fire. This is his simple statement of the doctrine of the Lord's return.

Augustine, who was one of the greatest men of the Christian Church of all time, lived A.D. 354–430. He at first adopted pre-millenarianism, but gave it up as 'carnal'. Augustine, says S. J. Case, laid 'the ghost of (pre-) millenarianism so effectively that for centuries the subject was practically ignored'.

4: *The reformers and the millennium*

IN expounding Revelation 20, Augustine explained the binding of Satan as the fulfilment of the words of Jesus: 'No man can enter into a strong man's house and spoil his goods unless he first bind the strong man.' The reigning of the saints with Christ he looked upon as a present actuality. His views were adopted very generally throughout the Church in the succeeding centuries. During the Middle Ages, Dr Shedd tells us millenarianism can hardly be said to have had any existence as a doctrine. About the year A.D. 1000 there was, to quote Shedd, 'an undefined fear and expectation among the masses that the year 1000 would witness the advent of the Lord'. This was not due to pre-millennial beliefs, but to a widely-held notion that the thousand years spoken of in Revelation 20 commenced with the first advent of Christ, and that the establishment of the Christian Church was 'the first resurrection'. So they expected A.D. 1000 would be the final close of history. A.D. 1000 passed, and those who had been throwing away treasures and abandoning estates as worthless, went to the opposite extreme of erecting massive structures, as if the present world were to last for ever.

When the Reformation came, millenarianism again appeared. It was an item in the belief of a wild and fierce sect of the Anabaptists. The Reformers set their faces against the teaching of this sect. The Augsburg Confession, drawn up by Melanchthon, approved by Luther and submitted to the Emperor and rulers of Germany as the confession of the Protestant faith, condemned millenarianism as a 'Jewish opinion', rejecting it along with the other Anabaptist notion of a limited future punishment.

The English 'Confession of Edward VI', from which the Thirty-nine Articles were afterwards condensed, also condemns millenarianism in these terms: 'Those who attempt to revive the fable of the millenarians oppose the sacred Scriptures and throw themselves headlong into Jewish absurdities.'

Calvin shows contempt for pre-millennial ideas when he says in the chapter on 'The Final Resurrection' in his *Institutes*, that Satan has endeavoured to corrupt the doctrine of the resurrection of the dead by various fictions, and adds: 'Not to mention that he began to oppose it in the days of Paul, not long after arose the Millenarians, who limited the reign of Christ to a thousand years. Their fiction is too puerile to require or deserve refutation.'

The Belgic Confession, which was widely adopted in Holland, Belgium, and Germany, guards the statement respecting the second advent of Christ by teaching that the time of its occurrence is unknown to all created beings, and that it will not take place *until the number of the elect is complete*. This guards against one of the worst features of the common pre-millenarian scheme, namely, that there will be people saved *after* Christ comes for His own.

The Second Helvetic Confession which was adopted in Switzerland, also in Scotland, Hungary, France, Poland, and Bohemia, speaks in very strong language: 'We reject the Jewish dreams that there will be before the Day of Judgment a golden age upon the earth, and that the pious will take possession of the kingdoms of the world, after their enemies, the ungodly, have been subdued.' The Confession then proceeds to quote Scripture against these 'Jewish dreams'. When at the Reformation men turned again to the Word of God, evidently they found no millenarianism there.

Let us turn, last of all, to the Larger Catechism of the Westminster Divines:

'We are to believe, that at the last day there shall be a general resurrection of the dead, both of the just and the unjust; when they that are then found alive shall in a moment be changed; and the self-same bodies of the dead which were laid in the grave, being then again united to their souls for ever, shall be raised up by the power of Christ. The bodies of the just, by the Spirit of Christ, and by virtue of His resurrection as their Head, shall be raised in power, spiritual, incorruptible, and made like to His glorious body; and the bodies of the wicked shall be raised up in dishonour by Him, as an offended Judge.

'Immediately after the resurrection shall follow the general and final judgment of angels and men; the day and hour whereof no man knoweth, that all may watch and pray, and be ever ready for the coming of the Lord' (Answers 87 and 88).

The Westminster Divines support this statement with a convincing array of Scripture proofs.

The historic Protestant position is not millenarian. It insists that the second coming of Christ is the signal for the final and general judgment.

5 : *The interpretation of Old Testament prophecy*

A PROPHET was an authoritative and infallible teacher of God's will. The common view that a prophet was one who foretold the future is incorrect. Certainly the prophets uttered predictions of things to come, but this was sometimes a comparatively small part of their work. A prophet was one who spoke for God, and such speaking included lessons of truth and duty, of faith and hope for the present, and the interpreting of the past, as well as the predicting of the future. This is evident if we consider the writings of Hosea, Jeremiah, Ezekiel, or any of the prophets. But in our present discussion we are taking the word 'prophecy' in its narrower sense of the foretelling of the future.

We have noted in chapter 2 that post-millenarians who look for a converted world before the Lord's coming (it is only fair to say that many post-millenarians do not) are not on sure ground, and that the pre-millenarian view of a millennium of earthly blessedness after Christ's coming is definitely ruled out by the New Testament. Those who hold to this latter view – that there will be a millennium of earthly blessedness after the Lord's coming – feel that they are in a very strong position when they appeal to the Old Testament. On the other hand, that great Old Testament scholar, Robert Dick Wilson of Princeton, used to say to some of his pupils, of whom the writer was one, that the Old Testament prophecies, instead of favouring the pre-millenarian view, were utterly against it. A study of Old Testament prophecy, in particular of parts of the book of Ezekiel, together with a fresh study of the New Testament Scriptures on the second coming, forced the present writer to abandon the pre-millenarian view.

Literalist View—Extravagant and Absurd

Pre-millenarians are usually strongly literalist in their view of Old Testament prophecy. They derive from it the notion that Christ will reign visibly and personally on a throne at Jerusalem over an Israel restored to Palestine; His reign will extend over the Gentile nations with the Jew, however, on top (Isa. 60:1–22), but with the nations yielding only a feigned obedience to His sway; during this time people who have mortal bodies will live in houses, eat of physical vineyards, bear children, be subject to sickness and death, though not to the same degree as at present (Isa. 65:20, 21); the temple and its services will be restored, with bloody sacrifices as sin-offerings to make atonement for the people (Ezek. 45:17); the temple priests will teach the people the difference between clean and unclean things (Ezek. 44:23); the tribes of the earth will come up to Jerusalem yearly to keep the feast of tabernacles; Christ will enter the temple by the eastern gate while the priests prepare His burnt-offering and peace-offering (Ezek. 46:2); and circumcision must again be practised under His reign (Ezek. 44:9).

Old Testament prophecy bears within itself a warning against such literalism. God said He would speak to the Old Testament prophets in dreams and visions and dark speeches (Num. 12:6–8; Hosea 12:10). So we may be prepared to find them using figurative speech and enigmatic language. The very first prophecy (Gen. 3:15) is couched in veiled and mysterious language. It uses figures of speech. As Luther said: 'It embraces and comprehends within itself everything noble and glorious that is to be found anywhere in the Scriptures.' It speaks of victory over the serpent under the figure of his head being bruised. Isaiah speaks of his overthrow by picturing him as having dust for food and the babe putting its hand on his den, and John portrays him as bound with a chain. Genesis and Isaiah and Revelation speak with one voice and give us glorious truth under these images.

Another early prophecy reads: 'God shall enlarge Japheth, and he shall dwell in the tents of Shem; and Canaan shall be his servant' (Gen. 9:27). Does 'he' in this text refer to God or Japheth; and if to Japheth, will the 'dwelling in the tents of Shem' be as conqueror or subject or friend; and whose servant will Canaan be – Japheth's or Shem's? The dwelling in the tents of Shem refers ultimately to the reception of Gentiles as well as Jews into the fold of Christ, but the language is enigmatic and a crass literalism would lead us astray.

When Ezekiel speaks of the people being restored to their own land, he gives us clear hints that we are not to take this literally. He says, 'David my servant shall be king over them' (37:24). If we take this literally, then David must be raised from the dead to feed the whole house of Israel and to rule over them – David, and not Christ. It will not do for the literalists to say that David here is the divine David, even Christ. They must be consistently literal.

Anyone who takes the trouble to follow the measurements given by Ezekiel of the restored temple and city and the divisions of territory among the tribes will find that these do not fit into the literal Palestine at all, and that they involve, if tried on the literal scale, the anomaly of water flowing uphill. It will not do in reply to say that all things are possible with God. God, in His Book, again and again asks us to believe things which are above reason, but never anything contrary to reason.

Ezekiel, in chapters 38 and 39, tells of Gog and all his hordes and many people with him coming up against Israel and covering the land as a cloud. He is completely overthrown. It takes all Israel seven years to burn the wood of his weapons, and all Israel are employed for seven months in burying his dead. Taking this literally, on a moderate estimate, it would involve an aggregate of 360,000,000 corpses. Then think of the pestilential vapours arising, the stench under the eastern sun, while such masses of dead awaited burial! As Patrick Fairbairn says, 'Who could live at such a time? It bids defiance to all the laws of nature; ... to insist on such a description being understood according to the letter is to make it take rank with the most extravagant tales of romance, or the most absurd legends of Popery' (*Ezekiel*, p. 423). The numbers 'seven years' and 'seven months' are without doubt symbolical; seven is the number of perfection, and what is emphasised is the completeness of the overthrow of the multitude of His people's enemies.

When Isaiah tells us that 'the mountain of the Lord's house shall be established in the top of the mountains and exalted above the hills', a literal interpretation would involve that the temple hill at Jerusalem be made higher than the Himalayas. The simple explanation, however, is that the elevation has long since taken place – when Christ appeared in the flesh, and the glory of the temple to which

He came was so enhanced that all that is great in the world shrank into insignificance in comparison. (Compare Haggai 2:9.)

Literalists often make much of the so-called unconditional promises of the land to Israel for ever, and of the throne to David's line. They should remember that God did say to one generation of Israel with regard to the possession of the land, 'Ye shall know My breach of promise' (see also 1 Samuel 2:30). In fact, as Fairbairn says, the promises could only be expected to meet with fulfilment as the Church (of Old Testament or New) is true to her calling (see Jeremiah 18:9, 10). If untrue and disobedient, then Israel became 'rulers of Sodom and people of Gomorrah' (Isaiah 1:10), and 'children of the Ethiopians' (Amos 9:7). As to the promise that there would not fail a man of his line to sit on his throne, David knew well that this promise had a conditional side. On his death-bed David quoted the Lord's word to him, '*If* thy children take heed to their way, there shall not fail thee a man on the throne of Israel' (1 Kings 2:4).

There were Old Testament prophecies which were fulfilled to the letter at Christ's first coming. There were others which pictured His ears being bored, His sinking in deep waters, dogs compassing Him about, and His being heard from the horns of the unicorns (wild oxen?). The bald literalist must hold that these are yet to be fulfilled, and that the Lord must yet suffer further humiliation.

Literalist View—Self-contradiction

We have shown that the literalist view of Old Testament prophecy will lead to much that is extravagant and absurd; we will now show that it leads to self-contradiction.

Ezekiel says four times over that in the day when Israel is restored, the office of the priesthood will be reserved for the sons of Zadok only (40:46; 43:19; 44:15; 48:11); Jeremiah declares that then all the Levites will be priests (33:18); while Isaiah affirms that God will take priests and Levites from all nations (66:20, 21). How can the literalist explain this?

Not only does the literalist view make one Old Testament prophet contradict another; it makes the Old Testament contradict the New. Ezekiel speaks of the temple rebuilt and of sacrifices for sin. According to the premillenarian there will be sacrifices again in the millennium. The Scofield Notes say, 'Doubtless these offerings will be memorial,' that is, merely commemoratory of Christ's great sacrifice at the cross. This will not do, however, for Ezekiel calls the sacrifices 'sin-offerings' and describes them as 'making atonement'. Now, the New Testament insists that the whole system of carnal ordinances is done away on account of the weakness and unprofitableness thereof. The handwriting contained in ordinances is for ever nailed to His cross. Of the law of ritual and sacrifice, we can say with Martin Luther that 'like Moses it is dead and buried, and let no man know where its place is'. 'A temple with sacrifices now would be the most daring denial of the all-sufficiency of the sacrifice of Christ, and of the efficacy of the blood of His atonement. He who sacrificed before, confessed the Messiah; he who should sacrifice now, would most solemnly and sacrilegiously deny Him' (Douglas's *Structure of Prophecy*, quoted in Fairbairn's *Ezekiel*, p. 442). We may add that when Jesus said, 'The hour cometh, when neither in this mountain, nor in Jerusalem, shall ye worship the Father,' He sounded the death-knell for all time of all merely localised worship.

If you are still puzzled because the prophecies of the rebuilding of the temple and the restoration to the land seem, on the face of them, to be literal, put the question to yourself – If the prophets had spoken of the New Testament Church, not under the figures of Israel of old, but in terms of New Testament grace and truth, would they have been understood? If they had heralded the glories of Christ's people, not under the figures of the land, the temple, and the sacrifices, but in the richness and fullness of New Testament language, it would have meant nothing and conveyed nothing to the Old Testament saints. They could not have borne such excess of light. Let us remember that when Christ did come, it was so difficult even for His chosen disciples to understand, and that He said to them, 'I have yet many things to say unto you, but ye cannot bear them now.' Only by things known, such as the land, the temple, and the sacrifices, could the prophets picture the unknown. The blessings which had marked the past would be the portion of the Israel of God more fully under the New Covenant. So David's reign, which had brought blessing and deliverance to Israel, is used to image forth a greater deliverance – 'My servant David shall be prince among them.' The evils which came upon them for their sins under the Old Covenant would be removed under the New. One of the greatest evils of Old Testament times was the division of Israel and Judah. So the blessed New Testament times are pictured to us under the figure of Israel and Judah reunited. Was not the Old Testament a typical dispensation?

It should be noted, in passing, that even in the New Testament traditional Jewish language about the kingdom of God is not avoided. At the close of Acts, for example, Paul's faith in Christ, which had brought him into bonds,

is described as 'the hope of Israel' (Acts 28:20). Old
Testament terms, such as 'the consolation of Israel', 'the
redemption of Israel', and 'the restoration of the kingdom
to Israel', are used with reference to Gentiles as well as
Jews (see Luke 2:25, 32).

The prophets frequently speak of the dooms upon
Edom, Philistia, Assyria, etc. The literalist holds that
these dooms are yet future. But where are the Edomites,
the Philistines, the Assyrians? Who can find them?
Zechariah foretold that the families of David, Nathan, and
Shimei would weep, every family apart (12:12-14). The
literalist holds that this is yet to be, but no one on the
face of the earth to-day can establish their descent from
any of these.

When we look at the vivid pictures of things future,
drawn often with circumstantial detail by the prophets, we
do well to remind ourselves of the condition of the prophets. They commonly prophesied in an ecstasy. Their
state was a supernatural one (see 1 Samuel 10:10-12).
Their mental faculties were not suspended, but, like Paul
when caught up to the third heaven, they might not be
able to tell if in the body or out of the body. In the prophets we read over and over such phrases as 'I was in the
Spirit and heard', 'the hand of the Lord was upon me',
'the Spirit of the Lord came upon me'. We must beware
of taking what they saw when in the supernatural state
with a bald literalism. Peter, when he was in an ecstasy or
trance, saw a vision – a sheet, and in it animals and creeping things and birds. Peter took a very literal view of what
he saw at first, but later he came to realise that it had a
spiritual significance. When the hand of the Lord was
upon Ezekiel, and he is told to enact this upon the stage,
namely, to lie on his side for 390 days and eat food cooked

with dung (4:9–12), we must beware of reading this too literally. So too when Hosea was told by God to take a wife of whoredom – a harlot; if we interpret this literally, we put a slur on the character of the good and holy God. As John Calvin says, if Hosea actually married such a wife as described, he ought rather to have hidden himself all his life than assumed the prophetic office.

To interpret the Old Testament prophecies with a uniform literalism, as many try to do, is to turn into a stone what the Lord meant for bread.

6: *The New Testament interpretation of Old Testament prophecy*

I<small>T</small> is objected to the non-millenarian view that it takes no account of Old Testament prophecy. We reply that the objector takes no account of the New Testament interpretation of Old Testament prophecy. The New Testament writers take prophecies which, from the literalist view, have to do with Israel, and apply them to the New Testament Church.

Old Testament Prophecies Applied to the Church

Let us here insist that there was a Church in Old Testament times; and that the Old Testament and New Testament believers form one Church – the same olive tree (Romans 11) – redeemed by the same precious blood and born of the same Spirit; and that the Old Testament prophets point directly and definitely to the New Testament Church. The contention of most pre-millenarians is that the out-calling of the Church of the New Testament was hid from the Old Testament prophets (this is the Scofield Bible view). They ask us to believe that the prophets who so clearly depict the person and offices and work of the Messiah, leave 'that next greatest, that complementary phenomenon, the rise and progress of the Holy Church throughout the world, entirely unrepresented on the prophetic page'. They ask us to believe that Christ came to establish a visible rule on this earth, but the Jews not being willing to accept the kingdom on Christ's terms, the offer was withdrawn and the kingdom postponed till His second advent. During the interval between the advents Christ established His Church, which is, they say, not a fulfilment in any sense of Old Testament promises and prophecies, but something new and unknown to the prophets – it is a 'parenthesis,' now amounting to well-nigh two thousand years, of which no word is clearly spoken by Old Testament prophecy. This is the view of H. A. Ironside. He says, 'The prophetic clock stopped at Calvary. Not one tick has been heard since.'

But, to our mind, to say that the Old Testament prophets do not speak of the Christian Church is outrageous, in view of many New Testament passages such as Romans 9:24–26, where we have Paul's statement that the calling out of Jew and Gentile in the Christian Church is the direct fulfilment of a prophecy of Hosea. In Acts 26:22 Paul claimed that he preached 'nothing but what the prophets and Moses did say should come' (R.V.). In Acts 2, Peter states that a prophecy of Joel is now (in these Gospel times) being fulfilled. Referring to the outpouring of the Holy Spirit, he says, 'This is that spoken by the prophet Joel: "And it shall be in the last days, saith God, I will pour out my Spirit upon all flesh".' The prophetic clock is evidently still ticking.

Times without number have we heard pre-millenarians scoff at the chapter-headings of our Authorised Version, such as:

Isaiah 30 – 'God's mercies towards his church.'
     ,,   34 – 'God revengeth his church.'
     ,,   43 – 'God comforteth the church.'
     ,,   44 – 'God's promises to his church.'

Isaiah 45 – 'Cyrus called for the church's sake.'
      ,,   50 – 'The ample restoration of the church.'
      ,,   54 – 'The church is comforted.'
      ,,   64 – 'The prayer of the church.'

Such headings are all wrong, say these pre-millenarians; they are a display of appalling ignorance on the part of those who inserted them; there was no Church in the Old Testament times, and to the prophets the New Testament Church was unknown. Yet Stephen spoke of a Church in Moses' time (Acts 7:38), and Paul says that believers of Old Testament and New form one olive-tree.

When Paul says (Eph. 3:5, 6) that it was not made known in past ages, *as* it hath now been made known, that the Gentiles should be fellow-heirs and of the same body, he does not at all say that this was utterly unknown to past ages, but rather that it was not known as fully and clearly as it is now (see also Romans 16:26).

St. Paul tells us that the Old Testament promise was made to Abraham and his seed; he quotes the promise, 'A father of many nations have I made thee,' and insists that this is fulfilled, not in the literal seed, but in the spiritual seed of Abraham (Romans 4). Those from his loins who walked in the steps of his faith, and all those not from his loins who shared his faith can call Abraham their father. This is Paul's way of looking at the Old Testament prophecies, and we are perfectly safe in following the apostle of the Lord.

In Galatians 3, Paul claims that the Old Testament prophecy to Abraham, 'In thee shall all the nations be blessed,' is fulfilled *now*, when God justifies the Gentiles by faith. In the light of such a statement as this, it is surely very bold and unjustified to declare that the Old Testament prophecies are silent as to the New Testament Church, and that there is no tick from the prophetic clock in this age.

Acts 15:13–18 is a very important passage in this discussion. Paul is attacked by some Jewish Christians for receiving believing Gentiles into the Church. A Council met at Jerusalem to deal with this specific matter, Peter and Paul being present. James, the leader of the Church at Jerusalem, says that this course of Paul's is no new thing, but was practised a considerable time before by Peter with express divine approval, as Peter himself had just stated. More than that, say James, this reception of the Gentiles was no afterthought in the divine plan, but was part of it from the beginning, as attested by the prophets. James proceeds to quote the prophets (mainly Amos), as follows: 'After this I will return and will rebuild the tabernacle of David that is fallen.' Amos was speaking of the judgments about to come upon Israel, and then gives this promise of God, 'I will rebuild the tabernacle of David.' James declares that this rebuilding of the tabernacle of David is now taking place in God's visiting the Gentiles to take out of them a people for His name. By the ingathering of the Gentiles, God is repairing the broken-down condition of the Old Testament Church. Remember that the whole subject under debate at the Council is the reception of the Gentiles into the Church and that James is quoting Amos's prophecy in favour of this reception. How absurd then for the Scofield Bible to hold that the Gentiles mentioned by Amos were not Gentiles of James's time, but of millennial times, two thousand years later! The Council was not discussing the prophetic map of the future, but a present and pressing problem. This problem was as to the reception of the Gentiles into the Church, and James quotes what Amos says as to the rebuilding of the tabernacle of David to justify the receiving of the Gentiles. He does this with the evident approval of Peter and Paul and the whole Council. In other words, in the view of the apostles, the tabernacle of David has become the living temple of the New Testament Church.

We have noted an admission from an unexpected quarter that James did apply Amos's prophecy to the Christian Church. In *The Witness*, the monthly magazine of the Open Brethren (March, 1944, issue), a writer states: 'It would also appear from Acts 15 that James had not travelled much farther (than the Old Testament writers to whom the mystery of Christ was not revealed), and thus quotes Amos as covering prophetically the opening of the door of faith to the Gentiles.' It is a gain indeed to see this admission that James does interpret Amos as foretelling the opening of the door of faith to the Gentiles in this present age; but surely it is very sad to see a belittling of apostolic authority from such a quarter.

In the Epistle to the Hebrews (chapters 8 and 10), we have the sacred writer claiming that the new covenant (of New Testament times) is the fulfilment of these words of Jeremiah: 'Behold, the days come, saith the Lord, when I will make a new covenant with the house of Israel and the house of Judah.' Israel and Judah are evidently the Israel of God, the New Testament Church. So the Authorised Version headings, which refer Old Testament prophecies to the New Testament Church, evidently have the support of the New Testament itself.

Our Lord Himself referred to the Old Testament prophecy of the coming of Elijah, and assured his hearers that 'Elijah is come' (in the person of John the Baptist –

Mark 9:12, 13). Yet some of the literalists are not satisfied; they say that Elijah is yet to come!

Zechariah prophesied, 'Behold, thy king cometh unto thee, . . . riding upon an ass, and upon a colt the foal of an ass, . . . and his dominion shall be from sea even to sea, and from the river even to the ends of the earth' (9:9, 10). Matthew quotes this passage (Zech. 9:9), and says it was fulfilled in the triumphal entry recorded in Matthew 21. The Scofield Bible takes the triumphal entry as a mere offer on Christ's part to be king; He did not really come as king. Yet Matthew declares He *did* come as king. Some literalists look for His riding on an ass into Jerusalem yet in the future, just because He did not come with the trappings of monarchy on the occasion described in Matthew 21.

In Acts 2:30, 31, Peter says of David, 'Being therefore a prophet, and knowing that God had sworn with an oath to him, that of the fruit of his loins he would set one upon his throne; he, foreseeing this, spake of the resurrection of Christ' (Revised Version). According to Peter, we do not need to wait till the millennium to have Christ on David's throne; He took that seat at His resurrection. This is confirmed by other Scriptures, which speak of Christ as already reigning (1 Cor. 15:25), possessed of all power in heaven and earth (Matt. 28:18), and having all things beneath His feet (Eph. 1:22). Let it not be objected that the eye of sense cannot behold Him clothed with the trappings of regal state as He governs earth's nations. By the eye of faith we see Him as our great High Priest within the veil; what hinders that in like manner we see Him as our King? 'We walk by faith, not by sight.'

No Future Jewish Kingdom

The New Testament has nothing to say about a return of the Jews to their own land, with Christ reigning on a throne at Jerusalem over a kingdom in which the Jews will have a national pre-eminence. Let it not be said that the New Testament does not deal with the Jews as a people – Paul does deal rather fully with the Jewish problem in Romans, chapters 9 to 11, and he has not a word to say about a future Jewish kingdom. Let it not be said that Paul had no motive or inducement to mention a future kingdom in which the Jews were to have national pre-eminence. Paul found that there were two stumbling-blocks to the Jews. One was the cross (1 Cor. 1:23). What the other was we can see from that occasion on which they listened to him till he spoke of being sent to the Gentiles (Acts 22:21), whereupon they raised a tremendous outcry – the second stumbling-block was the ingathering of the Gentiles. Now, if Israel's ancient glory was to be revived under the personal rule of Jesus Christ, surely Paul would have hastened to assure the Jews that there was the crown as well as the cross, and that it was only a matter of time till there would be a kingdom in which the Jews would have the foremost place and Jerusalem would be the metropolis of the world. So the stumbling-blocks would have been removed. The apostle, however, did not do this. On the contrary, he affirmed that the middle wall of partition between Jew and Gentile was broken down, and gave no hint that it would ever be restored. Believing Jews and Gentiles are one in Christ. The New Testament writers do not mention Christ reigning at Jerusalem on a secular throne; they are strongly insistent that He already reigns.

A leading pre-millenarian, L. S. Chafer, says that after

this gospel age there will be 'the re-gathering of Israel and the restoration of Judaism', and that there is 'an earthly people who go on as such into eternity, and a heavenly people who also abide in their heavenly calling for ever'; that is, God will have two distinct peoples, one on the earth and the other in heaven, for ever and ever. This may be consistent literalism, but surely it is a veritable delirium of folly.

The literalism which insists on the Old Testament prophecies being referred to the Israel after the flesh, is utterly inconsistent with the universal New Testament application of the promises to the spiritual seed. The New Testament insists that he is not a Jew who is one outwardly (Rom. 2:28, 29), that they are not all Israel which are of Israel (Rom. 9:6), that they that are Christ's are Abraham's seed (Gal. 3:29), that the blessing of Abraham has come upon the Gentiles in Christ Jesus (Gal. 3:14), and that there can be neither Jew nor Gentile (Greek), for 'ye are all one in Christ Jesus' (Gal. 3:28). The literalism that waits still for Christ to take His seat on David's throne at Jerusalem is inconsistent with Peter's announcement that Christ has already taken His seat on David's throne at His resurrection. The literalism which looks for a restoration of the temple at Jerusalem, with all nations coming to take part in its worship and its sacrifices for sin, is inconsistent with the New Testament assertion that such worship and sacrifice has been 'taken away' (Heb. 10:8, 9).

There were many Old Testament prophecies fulfilled to the very letter; others, very numerous too, were couched in figurative language, and the New Testament declares them to have been fulfilled, not in the exact letter, but in a spiritual sense.

Let it not be said that this makes it difficult to decide (as to prophecy yet unfulfilled) what to take literally and what spiritually. Everything of importance is clear; some details only the events themselves will make plain. So it was at Christ's first coming; so will it be with His second coming. Remember that it was an excess of literalism which led to the rejection of Jesus of Nazareth, and which has ever since confirmed the Jews in their unbelief. It was an excess of literalism on the part of His own disciples which frequently made them slow to grasp His meaning; for example, they took His warning, 'Beware of the leaven of the Pharisees,' to be a reproof to them for not bringing *loaves*. It was an excess of literalism which made the crowds carp at His reference to His atoning work, saying, 'How can this man give us his *flesh* to eat?'

The New Testament application of Old Testament prophecies compels us to assign an enlarged meaning and a spiritual significance to promises in which, at first sight, the Jew might seem to be exclusively interested.

7 : *Some general considerations from the New Testament*

ET us look at some strands which run through New Testament teaching, and also at a few of the terms used for the coming of the Lord.

Some New Testament Concepts

1. *The Last Days*. This expression is very often used of the whole Gospel age in which we now live. 'God hath in these last days spoken unto us by his Son' (Heb. 1:2). See also Acts 2:17; James 5:3; 1 Pet. 1:20. In Hebrews 9:26 we read, 'But now once in the end of the world hath he appeared to put away sin by the sacrifice of himself': here the whole Gospel age is looked upon as the end-time. In other words, the incarnation of Christ has introduced the final period in the world's history. Commenting on the words, 'It is the last time' (1 John 2:18), J. M. Ghysels remarks, 'It is not open to doubt that, according to Scripture, with the ascension of Christ and the descent of the Holy Spirit, the last period of the world's history has begun. This present period in which we live is the last on the divine programme.' If this present period is the last, then there remains nothing but the eternal state; there is no place left for a millennial age between.

2. *Already Citizens of Heaven*. Christ has ascended to the right hand of God, and believers, being vitally and mystically united to Him, are therefore with Him in a

spiritual sense, inhabiting the eternal world (heaven). See Ephesians 1:3; 2:6; Philippians 3:20; Colossians 3:1–3. The heavenly world and the earthly sphere are now parallel states, to both of which the believer belongs. As Dr Vos reminds us, the Christian has only his members upon earth, which are to be mortified; he himself belongs, and as a whole belongs, to the high mountain-land of the heavenly places above. This does not mean a toning down of his interest in the appearing of Christ. 'In reality', says Dr Vos, 'this whole representation of the Christian state as centrally and potentially anchored in heaven is not the abrogation, it is the most intense and practical assertion, of the other-worldly tenor of the believer's life.' He is already a heaven-dweller, but his soul will actually enter into the heavenly homeland at death, and at Christ's coming his body, as well as his soul, will actually inherit the eternal order, redemption being then at last complete.

Such is even now the Christian's position – he is a heaven-dweller. But turn to the picture given by Papias, and many others after him, of the millennium. Quoting a supposed statement of Christ, he said that in the millennium vines would grow 'having each ten thousand branches, and in each branch ten thousand twigs, and in each twig ten thousand shoots, and in every one of the shoots ten thousand clusters, and on every one of the clusters ten thousand grapes, and every grape when pressed will give twenty-five metretes (225 gallons) of wine. And when any one of the saints shall lay hold of a cluster, another shall cry out, "I am a better cluster, take me".' Grain, seeds, and grass would produce, Papias assures us, 'in similar proportions' to the vines. This description by Papias seems to be borrowed from the Jewish *Apocalypse of Baruch.*

Now, we feel that it is a genuinely Christian and Scriptural feeling which regards this sort of millennium as 'carnal'. It is a genuinely Christian and Scriptural sentiment to long rather to be for ever with the Lord in heaven. Those who are already citizens of heaven, and have such prospects of enjoying the full privileges of their citizenship, may well turn up their noses at ten thousand times ten thousand millennial grapes. Like the patriarchs, 'they desire a better country, that is *an heavenly*' (Heb. 11:16). Their affection is set on things above, not on things on earth (Col. 3:1, 2).

3. *The Two Ages.* The apostle Paul says that Christ is enthroned 'far above every name that is named, not only in this world (literally, age), but also in that which is to come' (Eph. 1:21). Under the expressions 'this age' and 'the one to come', the apostle groups all time, present and future, under Christ's sway. The Lord Himself used similar language; He promised to His faithful followers 'one-hundredfold now in this present time (age) and in the world (age) to come eternal life'. The age to come is evidently the eternal state, for in it there is 'eternal life'. Christ also spoke of the sin for which there is no forgiveness, 'neither in this age, neither in the coming one'. Here again it is plain that under these two ages Christ includes all time, present and to come. In Luke 20:34–36 we read, 'Jesus said, The children of this world (age) marry and are given in marriage: But they which shall be accounted worthy to obtain that world (age) and the resurrection from the dead, neither marry nor are given in marriage; neither can they die any more, for they are equal to the angels, and are children of God, being the children of the resurrection.' Yet again we see all time, present and to come, gathered up under the two expres-

sions 'this age' and 'that age', but here the dividing line between the two ages is also given – it is the resurrection of the dead, which all parties admit to take place at the coming of the Lord. (Yet Paul could speak of 'ages to come', just as we say 'while the endless ages roll'.)

The pre-millennial scheme maintains that there are three ages: (1) the present age, (2) the millennial age, and (3) the eternal state. The common New Testament representation is that there are but two ages, this Gospel one and the coming one, which is the eternal state; and the dividing line between the two is that momentous event, the second advent. We may note in passing that the New Testament says of this present age that it is an evil one (Gal. 1:4), so that we need hardly look for a wholly converted world within the bounds of Gospel times.

Some New Testament Terms

We will now look at some of the New Testament terms for the second coming. It may serve to clear the ground for our further studies.

One school of pre-millenarians distinguishes between 'the rapture' and 'the revelation', the former occurring at Christ's sudden and secret coming in the air to snatch away His saints, and the latter taking place after a seven-year interval of trouble following 'the rapture'. 'The revelation' would mark the beginning of the millennium. 'The rapture is solely Church truth,' says Dr Feinberg, a pre-millenarian; 'the revelation concerns all on the earth also.' Dr Feinberg also distinguishes between 'the day of Christ' and 'the day of the Lord', identifying 'the day of Christ' with 'the rapture', and 'the day of the Lord' with 'the revelation'. The Scofield Bible, which has been instrumental in gaining currency for these ideas, has the same views as Dr Feinberg. Its note on 1 Corinthians 1:7 is to the following effect:

These words are used in connection with the return of the Lord: (1) *Parousia*. The word simply means personal presence, and is used of the return of the Lord as that event relates to the blessing of the saints and the destruction of the man of sin. (2) *Apokalupsis* – 'unveiling', 'revelation'. The use of this word emphasises the visibility of the Lord's return.

Immediately following this note the Scofield Bible has another:

The 'day of Christ' relates wholly to the rewards and blessing of saints at His coming, as 'day of the Lord' is connected with judgment.

As a matter of fact, the word 'parousia' (which really means 'arrival') is used of the Lord's coming, not only as bringing blessing on the saints, *but also* judgment on the ungodly (see Matthew 24:37–39, where the coming, or parousia, is spoken of as bringing judgment like Noah's flood); while the word *apokalupsis* ('revelation'), which Feinberg applies to 'the day of the Lord', is used of the coming as the blessed hope of the saints in 1 Corinthians 1:7 and 2 Thessalonians 1:7.

Nor is it true that 'the day of Christ' relates wholly to the reward and blessing of saints. In Luke 17:24, 29, 30, Christ speaks of the day of the Son of man (surely the same as the day of Christ) bringing destruction like the day of Sodom.

Nor is 'the day of the Lord' connected solely with judgment. 'The day of the Lord' and 'the day of God' in 2 Peter 3 are clearly the same (even the Scofield Bible tacitly admits this); and that day is stated to be a blessed day, which believers are to 'look for and haste' (2 Peter 3:12), a day, moreover, bringing vast cosmical changes of heaven and earth. 2 Thessalonians 2 makes it further abundantly clear, that 'the day of the Lord' is to be identified with the parousia, or coming of the Lord, and so with 'the day of Christ'. It reads in part: 'We beseech you touching the coming of the Lord and our gathering together unto him, that ye be not soon shaken in mind or be troubled, . . . as that the day of the Lord is just at hand' (R.V. and A.S.V.). Here the coming of the Lord, or parousia, is clearly the same as the day of the Lord. The saints at Thessalonica thought that the blessed day of the Lord, when He would come for His own, was imminent. Paul, if he had held the pre-millennial scheme, would simply have replied, 'No, you're quite wrong. The day of the Lord will not come first. The day of Christ, or, to use another term, the parousia, must first come, and then, after a seven-year interval, the day of the Lord, or the revelation.' But he says nothing of the kind. He says 'the falling away will come first and the man of sin will be revealed whom the Lord will destroy with the brightness of His coming (parousia)' (verse 8) – the very same coming (parousia) with which is linked the gathering together of the saints (verse 1). Nothing could be clearer than that the day of the Lord and the coming of the Lord for His saints are one and the same, and that Antichrist must be revealed before the coming of the Lord (the parousia). The Scofield Bible makes a rather desperate effort to avoid this conclusion; it tries to get in the 'rapture' of the saints before the appearing of Antichrist. On 2 Thessalonians 2:7, 'He that now letteth will let, till he be taken out of the way, and then shall that wicked be revealed,' the Scofield note is: 'This person can be no other than the Holy Spirit in the Church, to be "taken out of the way".' Notice that the Scofield Bible says 'the Holy Spirit in the Church', meaning, of course, the Holy Spirit *and the Church*. This is hardly a fair way of dealing with Holy Scripture, for there is nothing whatever about the Church in verse 7. According to the Scofield theory, the Church must be got out of the way before Antichrist and the tribulation under him come, and by a piece of very forced exegesis the Scofield Bible reads the'rapture' into verse 7.

Dr Feinberg says that the first event (the rapture or day of Christ) has no signs to mark its approach, while the second event (the revelation or day of the Lord) has. It is surely directly contrary to the words of Christ in Matthew 24:29-33 to say that there will be no signs to mark the approach of the day of Christ's coming for His elect. Of course, there could not be very much surprise about the second event, if the pre-millenarian scheme were true, for once the 'day of Christ' came, the seven-year period of Antichrist and the great tribulation would follow. The seven-year period, once begun, would run its course to its close, when 'the day of the Lord', or 'the revelation' would follow. But good Greek students tell us that the word 'revelation' (*apokalupsis*) has intimately associated with it the very idea of suddenness and unexpectedness; yet according to the ordinary pre-millennial scheme, it can neither be sudden nor unexpected.

Suddenness and unexpectedness is to mark 'the day of the Lord', according to 1 Thessalonians 5:3, but according to this pre-millennial scheme, a seven-years' warning of its approach is given by that tremendously startling event, 'the rapture'.

Now, we will make bold to say that all efforts to distinguish these terms – 'coming', 'revelation', 'day of Christ', and 'day of the Lord' – have failed and are bound to fail. These terms are really interchangeable, and refer one and all to the great epochal event at the end of the world, when Christ will come to bless and reward His people, and to judge the world in righteousness.

8: *Christ's teaching as to His second coming*

The Parables

I̲N the parables of the wheat and tares and of the net (Matt. 13:24–30, 36–43, and 47–50), the Lord is giving, as all admit, a picture of this gospel age, which closes with His second coming. In the kingdom, the wheat and tares are to grow together till the harvest at the end of the world. Then the separation is to take place. All the children of the wicked one, represented by the tares, are to be eliminated from the scene. At the same time as doom comes upon the wicked, glory comes to the righteous – '*then* shall the righteous shine forth as the sun in the kingdom of their Father' (verse 43). This leaves no room for an earthly millennium. The present kingdom of the Son of man is followed by the eternal kingdom of the Father (as in 1 Cor. 15:24, 25). The wicked and righteous are together till harvest, and then there is complete and final separation. The end of this Gospel age brings to the wicked immediate and everlasting woe, and to the righteous everlasting glory. The Scofield Bible tries to avoid this conclusion by the following comment: 'The gathering of the tares into bundles for burning does not imply immediate judgment. At the end of this age the tares are set apart for burning.' It is a sufficient answer to quote the actual words of our Lord: 'As therefore the tares are gathered and burned in the fire; so shall it be in the end of this world. The Son of man shall send forth his angels, and they shall gather out

61

of his kingdom all things that offend and them which do iniquity; and shall cast them into a furnace of fire: there shall be wailing and gnashing of teeth' (verses 40–42). The question arises: Why is the Scofield Bible so anxious to keep the tares from the fire into which the Saviour represents them as cast? The answer is, that after the harvest at the end of the age the Scofield Notes teach that there is to be a millennial age, in which hosts of unregenerate people will be under the sway of Christ and His saints. The Saviour, however, asserts that there will be no unregenerate people to reign over, as at the end of this gospel age they are cast into the furnace of fire. The parable of the net also teaches that at the end of this Gospel age the wicked are to be cast into the furnace of fire (verses 49, 50). It is a very silly and unwarrantable proposition on the part of the Scofield Notes that the tares are kept in their bundles for a thousand years before the burning.

The parable of the pounds (Luke 19:11–27) shows how at the nobleman's return, faithful and unfaithful servants have their rewards apportioned, and he will say: 'Mine enemies, which would not that I should reign over them, bring hither, and slay them before me' (verse 27). This parable teaches that, when the Lord returns, He will not only reward His servants, He will also visit the wicked with their final judgment. His enemies will be 'slain', and there will be none left to yield what pre-millenarians call 'feigned obedience' in the supposed millennium.

The parable of the ten virgins is similar. It too indicates that the return of our Lord is the grand finale, the consummation of all things. One thing it makes perfectly clear – when the bridegroom comes, the door is shut (Matthew 25:10). One of the worst features in the teaching of many pre-millenarians is a second chance. They say that not till after His glorious appearing will the great body of the saved be brought to God. They hold forth a hope of salvation after the Lord has come for His own either during the tribulation period or in the millennium. Scripture teaches that when He comes for His own, the door will then be finally and for ever shut.

The parable of the talents (Matt. 25:14–30) has the same teaching. The coming of the Lord will bring glorious reward to His faithful ones, and at the same time terrible woe and condemnation to 'wicked and slothful servants'.

The Olivet Discourse

Have we not here the teaching of the 'rapture'? Do we not read here, 'One shall be taken, and the other left' (Matt. 24:40)? Notice, however, that in this passage we have no '*secret* rapture'. His coming is to be the very reverse of secret. It is to be as the lightning, it is to be visible, and the gathering of His elect will be 'with a great sound of a trumpet' (Matt. 24:26, 27, 30, 31). Notice, too, verses 37–40: 'As the days of Noah were, so shall also the coming of the Son of man be. . . . They knew not till the flood came, and took them all away; so shall also the coming of the Son of man be. Then shall two be in the field; the one shall be taken, and the other left.' Here there is not merely a comparison of Noah's day and Christ's; there is also a comparison of the results of these two days. In Noah's day some were taken to safety and others left to a terrible destruction; so shall it be at Christ's coming – some will be taken to safety and others left to an awful doom. That coming will bring destruction to the worldly and Christ-rejecting. Once again we point out that this leaves no place after Christ's coming for a millennium upon earth, in which unregenerate people will be under the sway of Christ and His saints.

The Judgment Scene of Matthew 25

All the nations are to be gathered before Christ's throne of glory, and there separated into sheep on His right hand and goats on His left; then to these are assigned respectively everlasting life and everlasting punishment. On the face of it this looks like a final and general judgment. But many pre-millenarians take it, as the Scofield Notes take it, to be a judgment of 'living nations' as nations. The test in this judgment, the Scofield Notes state, is 'the treatment accorded by the nations to the Jewish remnant, who will have preached the gospel to all nations during the tribulation'. W. E. Blackstone, the author of the pre-millenarian handbook, *Jesus is Coming*, was so impressed with the terrible plight of the Jews during the tribulation period, that he had boxes of Bibles stowed away in caves of Edom, where he expected the Jews would hide! It must suffice here to say that this interpretation of the term 'brethren' is certainly not in accord with Christ's definition of the word in Matthew 12:49, 50. (Compare Matthew 28:10.)

The whole question of the interpretation of this judgment scene hinges largely on the meaning of the expression 'all nations' (Matt. 25:32). Why should it mean anything other than what it means a few chapters later, 'Go ye, and teach all nations, baptizing them' (Matt. 28:19; cp. 24:14)? In Matthew 28:19 it means the whole human race; why should it mean something different in Matthew 25:32? In Romans 16:26, where Paul says that the mystery of the Gospel 'is made known to all nations', he means everyone in general; why should the expression mean anything else in Matthew 25:32?

The whole atmosphere of this scene shows that it is a judgment of individuals, not of nations as nations. Who ever would think of nations as nations being sent into everlasting punishment or everlasting life? (see Matt. 25:46). Who ever heard of nations as nations visiting the sick or the prisoner?

Moreover, it is worth noting that while the word 'nations' is a neuter noun (in Greek), the pronoun immediately following is masculine. 'Before him shall be gathered all nations (neuter), and he shall separate them (masculine) one from another, as a shepherd divideth his sheep from the goats.' The use of the masculine pronoun points to individuals rather than nations.

This judgment scene resembles strikingly that of Revelation 20:11–15 in the emphasis on the universality of it, and in the emphasis in both cases that the judgment is according to works – the outward works, of course, being evidence of inner faith. We have the same emphasis in the words of our Lord (Matt. 16:27), 'The Son of man shall come in the glory of his Father with his angels; and then he shall reward every man according to his works.' Also the same note is struck in the solemn words, 'The hour is coming, in the which all that are in the graves shall hear his voice, and shall come forth; they that have done good, unto the resurrection of life; and they that have done evil, unto the resurrection of damnation' (John 5:28, 29). At the same voice, heard at the same time, *all* shall come from the graves to judgment. None of His hearers could, by any stretch of imagination, have taken the Lord to speak of two judgments separated by a thousand years.

The so-called Athanasian Creed is an excellent summary of most of what we have gathered from our Lord's teaching: 'He ascended into heaven, he sitteth on the right hand of the Father, God Almighty: from whence he shall come to judge the quick and the dead. At whose coming all men shall rise again with their bodies, and shall give account for their works.'

Let no one say that all this discussion matters little. The idea of the wicked being summoned to the bar of God more than a thousand years later than the righteous, tends, to say the least, to lessen 'the terror of the Lord', a terror which the Scriptures again and again seem to associate with His coming at the last trump for the great and universal assize.

Moreover, when are those said to be saved in the millennium to be judged? The judgment of saints is past, and the judgment of the wicked is the only judgment then to come, according to the pre-millennial scheme.

Our Lord plainly teaches a general and universal judgment at His second coming. That coming will be visible and glorious. For the wicked it will mean final and irrevocable judgment. For the saints it will mean, not millennial bliss, but the very heaven of heaven itself as the seat of their abode – for did He not say, 'I go to prepare a place for you, and if I go and prepare a place for you, I will come again, and receive you unto myself; that where I am, there ye may be also' (John 14:2, 3)?

Let the saints rejoice. Let careless sinners and easy-going professors of religion be warned. Christ is coming, and the door will be shut. The sentence of eternal weal or woe will then be pronounced.

9: *The second coming in early apostolic preaching*

The Acts of the Apostles

IN the Acts of the Apostles we have a number of references to the Lord's return. In Acts 1 the disciples gazed at Him going 'as if carrying their eyes and hearts with Him' to heaven. Angels assured them He would come in like manner, that is, personally and visibly.

Acts 3:21 speaks of Christ 'whom the heavens must receive till the times of the restitution of all things'. The expression 'all things' does not mean absolutely all, for the Bible does not teach universalism. The incarnate but now glorified Son of God is in heaven, and there He must reside, this verse says, until 'the healing of all curable disorder and the restoration to communion with the Deity of all that He has chosen to be so restored' (J. A. Alexander's *Commentary on Acts*). It is necessary that He should so continue to reside, for there at the right hand of God He guides all things towards the glorious consummation when there will come the wind-up of the stupendous plan He is carrying into execution. His residence in heaven is an appointed means of its accomplishment. Peter, who is here speaking about 'the restitution of all things', is no doubt referring to the coming of the Lord, at which he says (in 2 Peter 3) there will be great world changes, the heavens and earth being burnt up, and a new heavens and earth ushered in. The returning Lord will do a thorough work, and there will be *no* sin and *nothing* 'out of joint' in the renovated earth.

In Acts 10:42, Peter says: 'He commanded us to preach and to testify that it is he which was ordained of God to be the Judge of quick and dead.' Christ is appointed to be the future Judge of all mankind – of all generations – past, present, and to come.

In Acts 17:30, 31, Paul says: 'But now (God) commandeth all men everywhere to repent: because he hath appointed a day in the which he will judge the world in righteousness by that man whom he hath ordained.' The judgment is to be a solemn judicial assize on all mankind at once. We are not going to enter into debate as to whether the day of judgment is to be an ordinary day of twenty-four hours. In this connection the statement of Augustine deserves consideration – 'God will cause it to be that to each man all his works, whether good or bad, will be recalled to memory, and seen with marvellous rapidity by the mental vision,' and so 'all will be judged at once and yet singly'. Certainly Paul's hearers would not have understood him to mean by a day a period of over a thousand years, with one judgment at its beginning and another at its close.

In Acts 24:15, Paul affirms that 'there shall be a resurrection of the dead, both of the just and unjust'. One resurrection, not two. The rising again of the dead is to be a general rising of all kinds and characters without exception.

The apostolic preaching has, as we would expect, the same testimony to bear with regard to the second advent as the Lord Himself. It is true to say, with Warfield, that Christ's coming for judgment was 'the very centre and substance of Paul's proclamation to the Gentiles'.

First Thessalonians

Let us consider next Paul's Epistles to the Thessalonians. They are not the first of his epistles in our English Bible, but they were the earliest written.

1 Thessalonians 4:13–18 is often quoted in support of the pre-millennial view. There is certainly nothing about a *secret* rapture in the passage, for there is no secrecy in 'a shout, the voice of the archangel, and the trump of God'. But the point sometimes made is, that because there is no mention here of the resurrection of the wicked, therefore it must differ in time from the resurrection of the righteous. In this passage, however, Paul is writing to comfort the sorrowing saints as to their believing friends who have died. Evidently, as in the Corinthian Church, there were some who doubted that the bodies of the dead in Christ would rise, and so they were in danger of sorrowing *even as* the heathen (verse 13). We must remember that this infant community had just emerged from heathenism. Paul writes to reassure them. 'For if we believe that Jesus died and rose again, even so them also which sleep in Jesus will God bring with him. For this we say unto you by the word of the Lord, that we which are alive and remain unto the coming of the Lord, shall not prevent (anticipate) them which are asleep. For the Lord himself shall descend from heaven with a shout, with the voice of the archangel, and the trump of God: and the dead in Christ shall rise first; then we which are alive and remain shall be caught up together with them in the clouds, to meet the Lord in the air; and so shall we ever be with the Lord. Wherefore comfort one another with these words.' When Paul says 'the dead in Christ shall rise first', the word 'first' expresses precedence, not with regard to the wicked but with regard to the living saints. He is assuring the

69

believers at Thessalonica that the dead saints, in gaining the presence of the Lord at His coming, shall not be one moment behind those who are alive. The wicked are not in view in these verses at all. These verses, let us repeat, were written to comfort believers who were sorrowing over their beloved dead who had died in the Lord. So the apostle's silence over the wicked is perfectly natural.

But is the apostle absolutely silent about the fate of the wicked? Read the passage which immediately follows. 1 Thessalonians 5:1–11 deals with the same subject as 1 Thessalonians 4:13–18. The fifth chapter is closely joined to the fourth chapter; it begins with the word 'but'. The fourth chapter answers the question: What about our beloved dead who have died in the Lord, at His coming? The fifth chapter deals with the question: What about the time of this great event? Many pre-millenarians posit a change of theme in chapter 5, for they distinguish 'the day of the Lord' from His coming for His saints. We have seen in a preceding chapter that no such distinction can be established. Certainly this passage does not indicate any. It is closely linked with what precedes: '*But* of the times and seasons, brethren, ye have no need that I write unto you, for yourselves know perfectly that the day of the Lord so cometh as a thief in the night. For when they shall say, Peace and safety: then sudden destruction cometh upon them, as travail upon a woman with child, and they shall not escape. But ye, brethren, are not in darkness, that that day should overtake you as a thief' (1 Thess. 5:1–4). Here the idea that the saints are snatched away several years before the day of the Lord is utterly demolished. Verse 4 says that that day has to do with the saints also, but that it should not take them unprepared as a thief tries to do.

Moreover 1 Thessalonians 5 shows us that the day of the Lord's second advent brings doom to the wicked. Paul associates with the second coming both the resurrection and ensuing glory of the saints *and* the sudden destruction of the wicked. Without the shadow of a doubt, 'that day' has its reference to both parties: – believers are to look for it (1 Thess. 5:4–10), for *then* they shall obtain salvation in all its fullness (verse 9), *then* they shall 'live together with Him' (verse 10); while that *same* day will bring the false security of unbelievers to an end in their 'sudden destruction'.

Second Thessalonians

In 2 Thessalonians 1, to comfort is still the apostle's object. In this case the comfort is needed because of persecutions and tribulations. Paul urges that their trials are a token of the Lord's favour, and by them God shows that He counts the tried ones worthy of the kingdom. But God will 'recompense tribulation to them that trouble you; and to you who are troubled rest' (2 Thess. 1:6, 7). When will He recompense tribulation to the one party and rest to the other? He immediately gives the answer, '*when* the Lord Jesus shall be revealed from heaven with his mighty angels, in flaming fire taking vengeance on them that know not God'. Will the sentence be executed on the righteous and the wicked at the same time? The apostle repeats the answer, Yes. For he goes on to say, 'they that know not God and obey not the gospel of our Lord Jesus shall be punished with everlasting destruction'. When? He gives the answer, '*when* he shall come to be glorified in his saints, and to be admired in all them that believe' (verse 10).

We may notice that when the Saviour comes for the

deliverance of His troubled saints, He comes 'in flaming fire' – no *secret* rapture here! But it is even more important still to notice how the reward of the righteous and the punishment of the wicked are interwoven with each other *as to time*, and made to follow, both of them, immediately on the coming of the Lord.

Surely this passage should make perfectly clear that there is no secret rapture to be followed at an interval of several years by an open revelation of the Lord and His glory to the world.

Surely it is perfectly clear also that since the coming of the Lord brings upon the wicked 'eternal destruction away from the face of the Lord', there are no wicked who will survive His coming to be ruled over in a millennium to follow. But there must be wicked people surviving, according to the pre-millennial scheme. And even at the very close of the millennial reign there are wicked in number as the sand of the sea (Rev. 20:8), according to the pre-millennial scheme of interpretation.

This passage in 2 Thessalonians should settle once and for all the question of there being two resurrections separated by a thousand years and more, at the first the righteous receiving blessing and reward, and at the second the wicked experiencing His wrath and vengeance. It is clear that here is set forth one great consummating event. It is *one event* which is spoken of, and this one event has two accompaniments – rest for God's people and tribulation for their adversaries. The apostle very evidently regards the general resurrection and final judgment as taking place at the coming of the Lord.

It is hard to see, supposing Paul were writing expressly to refute the notion of a *divided* judgment, how he could have done so more plainly than in this passage.

10: *The victory over death*

IN 1 Corinthians 15:22–27 we read: 'For as in Adam all die, even so in Christ shall all be made alive. But every man in his own order: Christ the firstfruits; afterward they that are Christ's at his coming. Then cometh the end, when he shall have delivered up the kingdom to God, even the Father; when he shall have put down all rule and all authority and power. For he must reign, till he hath put all enemies under his feet. The last enemy that shall be destroyed is death. For he (God) hath put all things under his (Christ's) feet. But when he saith all things are put under him, it is manifest that he is excepted, which did put all things under him.'

The pre-millenarian interpretation of this passage is as follows: Verses 23 and 24 give three stages of resurrection, (*a*) Christ's resurrection, (*b*) the resurrection of His saints at His coming, and (*c*) 'the end' of the resurrection, that is, the resurrection of the wicked. Between (*b*) and (*c*) the pre-millenarian puts more than a thousand years, the actual thousand years itself being the millennium. The kingdom which Christ gives up to the Father at 'the end' is His millennial kingdom. In this kingdom He abolishes all adverse rule, and puts all enemies beneath His feet, the last to be subdued being death.

This is a plausible interpretation, but let us examine it. First, let us notice that Scripture does not say 'the end

73

or the resurrection', but simply 'the end'. Where this expression 'the end' occurs, it means the end of all things, or the end of the world. It is certainly a straining of the word to press it into another groove here, and to make it mean 'the end of the resurrection'.

The word 'then' in the phrase 'then cometh the end' does not necessarily imply an interval between the resurrection of the saints and 'the end'; it is often used of immediate sequence. Many pre-millenarians admit this. Also let us notice that the word 'cometh' has no equivalent in the Greek, so that the phrase is just 'then the end'.

To the pre-millenarian who reads into the passage a resurrection of the wicked more than a thousand years after Christ's coming, we reply that the introduction of the wicked is entirely irrelevant. Paul's whole effort in this chapter is to show that those who are Christ's will rise from the dead at His coming or, if they are still alive then, they will share in the glorious transformation to be wrought by that event. It is only those 'in Christ' who come into view, as in 1 Thessalonians 4. And the words 'then the end' in verse 24 simply mean that the resurrection of the righteous and the grand finale, the very last end, fall together. This is strongly supported by the expression 'the last trump' in verse 52. This trump sounds at the resurrection of the saints, and the prospect of any further crisis is excluded. The last trump *is the last*.

Let us note again the order of events in the pre-millenarian scheme of things in 1 Corinthians 15:

(*a*) Christ raised.

(*b*) Believers raised at the close of the Gospel age.

(*c*) Then ensues (after a short period of tribulation, according to most pre-millenarians) the millennial kingdom of Christ, during the course of which He overthrows all hostile powers and puts all things under His feet, the last of these being death. The whole millennium will be occupied with this work of conquest. The Scofield Notes on 1 Corinthians 15 state: 'The Kingdom of heaven, thus established (in the millennium) under David's divine Son, has for its object the restoration of the divine authority in the earth, which may be regarded as a revolted province. . . . When this is done, the Son will deliver up the kingdom (of heaven) to God, even the Father, that God (the triune God) may be all in all.'

(d) At the close of the millennium there will be a short period in which Satan is let loose, and will lead a host as the sand of the sea in number from the four quarters of the earth. Then follows 'the end', which the pre-millenarian interprets to mean the end of the resurrection, its last stage, that is, the resurrection of the wicked.

A question immediately arises – if the glorious Saviour has reigned for a thousand years and put all things, even to the last enemy, beneath His feet, where are the hosts of evil 'in the four quarters of the earth' to come from at the close of the thousand years? To that question the premillenarian has no satisfactory answer.

But what we want to look at particularly now is this kingdom in verses 24 and 25, in which Christ abolishes all rule and authority and power. When does it begin and when does it end? We have seen that the pre-millenarian makes it begin after Christ's second coming for His people and last for a thousand years. Is this so? We for our part believe it is easy to fix upon the end of this kingdom which Christ gives up to the Father. Having fixed the end, we will then possibly be able to fix the beginning. We agree with the Scofield Notes that it seems to be indicated that the conquests of this kingdom mentioned in verses 24 and

25 will take some time; witness the expressions, 'He must reign *until* . . .' and 'the *last* enemy'. At length, however, the last enemy, death, will be abolished, and then, all things being subjected to Christ, He shall deliver up the kingdom to God, even the Father (verses 26 and 28). So death is the last enemy, and when it is abolished this kingdom ends. But verse 54 tells us when death is abolished. It is abolished when the dead are raised incorruptible and the living are changed; and the dead are raised and the living changed at Christ's coming. *Then* death is swallowed up in victory. 'The spectacle of multitudes, untouched by death, receiving their perfect and immortal bodies is the great pageant of the conquest of death.'

What kingdom is this which thus terminates at the coming of Christ to raise His saints? The Scriptures teach, as Charles Hodge points out in his Commentary on 1 Corinthians 15:24, a three-fold kingdom of Christ:

'(1) That which necessarily belongs to Him as a divine person, extending over all creatures, and of which He can never divest Himself.

'(2) That which belongs to Him as the incarnate Son of God, extending over His own people. This also is everlasting. He will for ever remain the head and sovereign of the redeemed.

'(3) That dominion to which He was exalted after His resurrection, when all power in heaven and earth was committed to His hands. This kingdom which He exercises as the God-man, and which extends over all principalities and powers, He is to deliver up when the work of redemption is accomplished. He was invested with this dominion in His mediatorial character for the purpose of carrying on His work to its consummation. When that is done, that is, when He has subdued all His enemies, then He will no longer reign over the universe as mediator, but only as God; while His headship over His people is to continue for ever.'

We have seen that this mediatorial kingdom is to end at His coming when the last enemy, death, is abolished. When does it begin? Paul, in Colossians 2:15, tells us that Christ triumphed by His cross over principalities and powers (the same Greek words as are translated 'rule' and 'authority' in 1 Corinthians 15:24). So the victory was in principle won at Calvary and on that first Easter morning; and Christ must reign on high till this victory is completely carried into effect (verse 25). We can now fix the beginning of this kingdom at Christ's resurrection. Compare Matthew 16:28; Mark 9:1; Luke 9:27. It was the risen Saviour who was made both Lord and Christ (Acts 2:36); it was He who was exalted to be a Prince (Acts 5:31); it was He who could say, 'All power is given unto me in heaven and in earth' (Matt. 28:18).

Christ's kingdom, which He possesses as mediator, is then already in existence. At His coming again the last enemy will be abolished, and He will give up His mediatorial kingdom to the Father. Then the kingdom of God in the fullness of its glory will be ushered in (verse 50). Into this kingdom in its perfect state flesh and blood cannot enter in their present weak and 'fleshly' state; only the glorified saints with their glorified bodies can inherit the kingdom of God (verses 50–54). But pre-millenarians distinguish the kingdom of Christ, which they say is the millennial kingdom, from the kingdom of God, which they say is the eternal state. According to their scheme of things, the glorified saints, after the coming of the Lord, should enter into the millennial kingdom of Christ. We have just shown, however, that they do actually enter (see verses 50–54) the kingdom of God in all its glory; that is, they enter the eternal state, not the millennium. (Compare Matt. 13:39, 41, 43.)

Even a casual reading of 1 Corinthians 15:22–28 does confirm this – that Christ's kingdom here referred to is already in existence. And it is established beyond the shadow of a doubt that this kingdom is not a millennial kingdom after Christ's coming, but His kingdom as mediator which comes to an end with the raising of His saints, when He delivers them finally and for ever from the last vestiges of death's sway. Then death is swallowed up in victory, and the cry will arise, 'O death, where is thy sting. O death, where is thy victory?' (verse 55, R.V.).

It is in accord with this view of the kingdom of verse 24 as a present kingdom that Christ is pictured in Ephesians 1:21 as *already* seated far above all rule and authority.

How glorious it is that Christ reigns even now! And 'He must reign till he hath put all enemies under his feet.' 'Then is the end,' the glorious consummation of all things.

> *Jesus the Saviour reigns,*
> *The God of truth and love;*
> *When He had purged our stains,*
> *He took His seat above:*
> *Lift up your heart, lift up your voice;*
> *Rejoice; again I say, Rejoice.*

11 : *New heavens and a new earth*

The Epistle to the Romans

IN Romans 2:3–16 we read: 'Thinkest thou, O man, that judgest them which do such things, and doest the same, that thou shalt escape the judgment of God? . . . But after thy hardness and impenitent heart treasurest up unto thyself wrath against the day of wrath and revelation of the righteous judgment of God; who will render to every man according to his deeds: to them who by patient continuance in well-doing, seek for glory and honour and immortality, eternal life: but unto them that are contentious, and do not obey the truth, but obey unrighteousness, indignation, and wrath, tribulation and anguish, upon every soul of man that doeth evil, of the Jew first and also of the Gentile; but glory, honour, and peace, to every man that worketh good, to the Jew first and also to the Gentile; for there is no respect of persons with God. For as many as have sinned without law shall perish without law: and as many as have sinned in the law shall be judged by the law; . . . in the day when God shall judge the secrets of men by Jesus Christ according to my gospel.'

Beyond all question it is the final judgment which is here spoken of, and even the resurrection of the righteous is implied when those who have sought for immortality are spoken of as receiving it in 'eternal life'. Paul teaches here that the judgment of righteous and wicked is simultaneous.

'In the day when God will judge the secrets of men by Jesus Christ' two things are to happen – those who have sought for glory and honour and immortality will receive eternal life and upon those who have been disobedient will come indignation and anguish. David Brown says, 'This passage is singularly decisive. Observe the alternation from righteous to wicked, and from wicked to righteous, in the description of one and the same day of judgment.' Bishop Waldegrave says, 'It instructs us, with a studied distinctness of reiterated statement, that as there shall be a simultaneous arraignment, so there shall also be a simultaneous trial of the just and the unjust, without the exception of a single individual, at the bar of eternal judgment.'

It will not do for the pre-millenarian to take 'the day' here spoken of as over a thousand years in length, with judgment at its beginning and at its close, quoting in support the text 'one day is with the Lord as a thousand years'. As Bishop Waldegrave suggests, '*We* might with equal propriety maintain that the remaining portion of the text, "and a thousand years as one day", gives the right interpretation of the millennium of Revelation 20.' Paul, in Romans 2, and his Master, in Matthew 25, speak with one voice in declaring the simultaneous judgment of all mankind. The apostle describes one closely unified event, at which the destinies of all are finally and for ever decided.

The First Epistle of Peter

In 1 Peter 1 we read that God's elect people have a 'living hope' of 'an inheritance, incorruptible and undefiled, and that fadeth not away, reserved in heaven' for them (1 Peter 1:3, 4). The millennial inheritance about which many are so enthusiastic, is not without an admixture of evil – a very considerable admixture of evil which manifests itself at the close of the millennium in a rebel host full of hellish malice. This millennial inheritance is earthly and is of limited duration. But the inheritance to which Peter calls the believer's attention has absolutely nothing that defiles, nothing that mars; its blessedness is eternal and it is 'in heaven'. No wonder Peter exhorts believers to 'set their hope to the full upon the grace that is to be brought unto them at the revelation of Jesus Christ' (1 Peter 1:13); for at Christ's appearing the whole ransomed Church will be taken to be for ever with the Lord in the heavenly mansions to which neither world nor flesh nor devil have access.

The Second Epistle of Peter

In 2 Peter 3 the apostle sets out to remind his readers of well-known truths. He does this because there will arise scoffers, who will mock at the doctrine of Christ's return, saying: 'Where is the promise of his coming?' These mockers reason that the world will go on always as it has done in the past. Peter says this will not be so. 'The heavens and earth, which are now,' he says, 'are kept in store, reserved unto fire against the day of judgment and perdition of ungodly men. . . . The Lord is not slack concerning his promise, . . . The day of the Lord will come as a thief in the night; in the which the heavens shall pass away with a great noise, and the elements shall melt with fervent heat, the earth also and the works that are therein shall be burned up. Seeing then that all these things shall be dissolved, what manner of persons ought ye to be in all holy conversation and godliness, looking for and hasting (unto) the coming of the day of God, wherein the heavens

81

being on fire shall be dissolved, and the elements shall melt with fervent heat? Nevertheless, we, according to his promise, look for new heavens and a new earth, wherein dwelleth righteousness. Wherefore, beloved, seeing that ye look for such things, be diligent that ye may be found of him in peace, without spot, and blameless' (2 Peter 3:7-14). Note the following points about this passage:

1. Peter is giving no new teaching; he expressly says he is repeating well-known truths taught by prophets and apostles. Peter follows the Lord Jesus and Paul in using the figure of the Lord's coming 'as a thief' (compare 2 Peter 3:10, Matt. 24:42-44, and 1 Thess. 5:2).

2. The 'day of the Lord' and the 'coming' of the Lord are one and the same. Notice the connection. Scoffers will say: 'Where is the promise of his coming?' to which Peter replies, 'The Lord is not slack concerning his promise. . . . The day of the Lord will come,' and he adds, 'we, according to his promise, look for new heavens and a new earth'. Scoffers may mock at 'the promise of his coming', but Peter assures us twice over that *that promise* will most certainly be fulfilled, in the coming of the day of the Lord and in the ushering in then of new heavens and a new earth. Notice, too, that while the Lord spoke of His *coming* as thief-like, Peter speaks of 'the day of the Lord' as thief-like. This is a fresh indication that the 'coming' and 'the day of the Lord' are the same.

3. At this 'coming', or 'day of the Lord', there is to be a great conflagration. A very strong Greek word is used of the 'burning up' of heaven and earth – a word indicating a 'thorough' burning. There will be great cataclysmic changes at the coming of the Lord. There will be a new heaven and a new earth, the first heaven and the first

earth passing away. He that sits on the throne will say, Behold, I make all things new.

This does not fit in with pre-millennial doctrine, according to which Jesus will come to reign at Jerusalem over pretty much the same old world. According to 2 Peter, there will be no 'old world' left after His coming. And surely the Christian heart delights to think that it is not over the old sinful world which rejected Him, but over a new world, that He comes to reign.

4. This destruction of heaven and earth will be unexpected – 'the day of the Lord will come as a thief in the night, in the which the heavens shall pass away and the earth be burned up'. The late Rev James Hunter, quoting this text, gave a strong rebuke to pre-millenarians who 'say that the Bible is to them infallibly true, and yet affirm with the godless scientists that the earth will last for hundreds of years – for more than a thousand years'. If the pre-millenarian scheme were correct, then the dissolution of the earth must yet be far away, and cannot come upon us unexpectedly.

5. At Christ's coming there will appear a new heaven and a new earth in which there is *absolute perfection* (2 Peter 3:13). James Hunter once said, 'It would seem as if the devil had torn the third chapter of 2 Peter out of the Bible of some Christians to-day.' He was thinking of the ideas abroad about an earthly kingdom after Christ's coming, a kingdom peopled to a considerable extent by unregenerate men and women left over at Christ's coming for this purpose; a kingdom which a pre-millenarian commentator (Walter Scott) admits to be 'at the best an imperfect condition'. Mr Hunter went on to affirm that Christ, when He comes, will have no need to look round for people to populate the new world. They will be at

hand in the persons of His own redeemed. 'Lawlessness', said Mr Hunter, 'will not exist in that world. . . . The curse being removed, and sin which occasioned the curse, "there will be nothing to hurt or destroy in all God's holy mountain".' In the new heaven and new earth, says Peter, there 'dwelleth righteousness'. The renovated universe will partake of the nature of heaven.

In Romans 8:21 we are told that the creature (creation) itself shall be delivered from the bondage of corruption into the glorious liberty of the children of God. Paul goes on to say that not only creation, but 'we ourselves groan within ourselves, waiting for the adoption, to wit, the redemption of our bodies'. All nature, now groaning under the curse pronounced at the Fall, awaits a deliverance and renovation corresponding to the deliverance of the redeemed. This deliverance for which creation waits cannot be the millennium, for sin still remains in the millennium, though held in check by Christ's rule. It is 'the glorious liberty (literally, the liberty of the glory) of the children of God', into which creation longs to enter. This glorious liberty, experienced at the redemption or resurrection of the body, is a state of absolute perfection. We can see that Paul, in Romans 8:21, 23, and Peter in his second epistle, both refer to the same great change or 'fiery bath', from which new heavens and a new earth will emerge, fitted to be the abode of the glorified saints.

6. Peter urges believers, in view of the impending dissolution of heaven and earth at Christ's coming, to 'look for and haste the coming of the day of God, wherein the heavens being on fire shall be dissolved, and the elements shall melt with fervent heat'. The day of the Lord and the day of God are manifestly the same, as what happens on the one is said to happen on the other also (verses 10 and

12). The great event of which Peter speaks is one for which Christians are to be earnestly on the watch, and in view of it, they are to be holy. It is to be a great day for them.

7. Evidently that day will be a dread day, a day of judgment and perdition (verse 7) for unbelievers. Coming as a thief, it will take them unprepared. It is perfectly plain from verses 7, 10–12 that the day of 'destruction' of the heavens and the earth by fire is at once 'the day of judgment and perdition of ungodly men', and the glad day for which Christians are to look.

This passage (2 Peter 3) leaves no place for a millennium into which unsaved people will pass after the second coming to enjoy something of the millennial bliss. There will be no room for evil, even though it be evil held in check, in all the wide domain of God's resurrected, glorified saints. They will inherit, says Peter, a new heaven and earth, where righteousness alone dwells.

We will now come to the book of Revelation; but let us review the teaching of the Gospels, the Acts, and the Epistles. We have seen that nowhere is it taught that the second coming will usher in a provisional kingdom, in the glories of which resurrected saints, with their glorified bodies, will share with sinners. The unanimous testimony of the Lord and His apostles is that the second coming will bring complete doom to sinners, and everlasting bliss in the eternal state to believers; and from that state of bliss sin will be utterly and for ever excluded.

Robert Strong, from whose articles in *The Presbyterian Guardian* on this subject we have received many suggestions, sums up New Testament teaching on the second coming thus: 'The Lord returns to a world that is still hostile to His Gospel and His rule over it; He resurrects the bodies of departed saints, and translates them and His living saints to be with Him; He consumes Antichrist and his rebel followers in a fiery overthrow that engulfs also the world; He sets up the throne of His judgment, and summons before it both men and angels, that justified men may be publicly acquitted and acclaimed to be His own, that wicked men and rebel angels may be shown justly destined to everlasting perdition; He establishes new heavens and a new earth to be the abode of righteousness for ever.'

May we who believe, seeing we look for these things, give all diligence that we may be found in peace, without spot, and blameless in His sight! May others be aroused to seek the Lord while He may be found!

12: *Three views of Revelation*

T̲HE interpreters of Revelation may be grouped in three main schools, according to the answer they give to the question: To what period of time do the visions and events of the book belong? If they answer 'time past', they are preterists (Latin, *praeter* – past); if they answer 'time future', they are futurists; and if they answer that they view the book as 'comprehending' in its scope the entire history of Christ's kingdom, they are what N. B. Stonehouse has termed 'comprehensivists'.

The Preterist

The Preterist holds that the book has in view, primarily at least, events contemporaneous with the apostle or imminent when he wrote. The prophecies in it had their fulfilment by the time of Constantine, that is, by the early part of the 4th century A.D. A Jesuit, Alcasar (A.D. 1614), was the father of this school.

The Book of Revelation bears on the face of it indications which forbid us to confine it to the days of the Cæsars. As William Milligan states: 'It treats of much that was to happen down to the very end of time, down to the full accomplishment of the Church's struggle, the full winning of her victory, and the full attainment of her rest. . . . There is a progress in the book which is only stopped by the final advent of the Judge of the whole earth' (*Lectures on The Apocalypse*, p. 141). The Preterist interpretation would resolve Revelation into a handbook of the history of the Church under the Cæsars. It is plain that it has much wider scope and usefulness.

The Futurist

The Futurist holds that the book has in view, primarily at least, the climactic events centring around the return of our Lord. This view postpones the real importance of most of the book, in its primary reference at any rate, to a short period at the end-time. The Jesuit Ribera (A.D. 1603) was the father of this school. John Darby, among others, adopted futurist views and these are widely held to-day. Most pre-millenarians are futurists. Walter Scott, in his commentary on Revelation, gives the common futurist view: 'Chapters 2 and 3 unfold the moral history of the Church in successive periods of her history, from the close of the first Christian century. . . . In chapters 4 and 5 heaven, and not earth, is the scene of action, the heavenly saints having been removed to their home above. . . . We place the Rapture of the saints *after* the Church ruin shown in chapter 3, and before the glory witnessed in chapter 4.' Scott goes on to say that 'events under the Seals, Trumpets, and Vials transpire *after* the Rapture and *before* the Appearing in glory'. He adds: 'It will be impossible to understand the Revelation if this is not clearly seen.' How can it be 'clearly seen' when there is not the slightest hint of a 'Rapture' between chapters 3 and 4, and no hint anywhere that the Letters to the Seven Churches in chapters 2 and 3 indicate seven 'successive periods' in the Church's history?

D. G. Barnhouse, in his exposition of the Apocalypse, says: 'The one principle of study . . . is that the major portion of this book belongs entirely outside of the age of the Church, and that regathered Israel is the centre of the scene, and that the Church does not even appear in the discussion.' Thus this amazing futurist theory asks us to believe that the Book of Revelation for the most part has nothing to do with the Church, her trials and conflicts and triumphs. Philip Mauro, who was himself once a futurist, surely had good right to object that this theory 'tends to quench one's interest in this wonderful book, by pushing the things it predicts far away from us, making its trans-cendently important revelations to be for those of a coming dispensation, the so-called "tribulation saints", and thus virtually detaching it from the rest of the Bible.' Mauro adds: 'On an occasion some years ago, when I raised a question about this with one who held the futurist view, he suggested that we should not grudge to the "tribulation saints" one book out of the sixty-six of the Bible. But I do most decidedly grudge it to them, and the more so because I am firmly persuaded that the "tribulation saints" of the futurist system are altogether an imaginary company; and that we, the Lord's people of this dispensation, are the true "tribulation saints" (John 16:33; Acts 14:22).' It would have been cold comfort, surely, for the saints of John's time, many of them like John himself suffering under the Emperor Domitian, to be given a book almost altogether concerned with the men of millenniums later.

The Comprehensivist

The Comprehensivist (or Historical) view claims that the book does not deal with some limited phase of Christ's kingdom at its beginning (as does the preterist) or at its close (as does the futurist), but with the grand sweep of the history of that kingdom from the First Advent to the

Consummation. In this view are included (*a*) the Church historical school, (*b*) the continuous-historical, and (*c*) the kingdom historical.

The Church historical school takes the book as setting forth the chief phases of Church history. This point of view began to appear in the early centuries. Early writers on the subject were futurists only in that they held that the visions of Revelation were just beginning to be fulfilled in their time. They believed that the things foretold were in the making in their days and did not belong merely to the end of the age. Luther and the Reformers in general belonged to this school, and later writers, like Bishop Wordsworth (1807–1885), have followed in their steps.

The continuous historical view differs from the Church historical mainly in that it interprets the book as history *without a break*; there is no overlapping of the visions; the seals follow one another in chronological sequence – the seventh seal comprehends within itself the seven trumpets; the trumpets follow one another in time; and the seventh trumpet comprehends within itself the seven vials. So from the first seal to the seventh vial is history without interruption from the beginning to the end of the Gospel era. Many of those who hold this view estimate that we are in the days of the seventh vial, and so near the consummation.

The kingdom historical school is sometimes called the 'symbolical' or 'spiritual' or 'philosophy of history' school. On the whole the term 'kingdom historical' is to be preferred. This school does not take the book as a continuous and unbroken record of Church history, nor even in the strict sense as a précis of Church history. It does take the book as 'concerned with the broad sweep of the unfolding of the kingdom of God to its great climax in the second advent' (N. B. Stonehouse).

These three historical views have this in common – that they regard the Book as comprehensive of the entire history of the kingdom of Christ. In favour of the comprehensivist view of Revelation, it may be urged that it is in accord with the rest of the New Testament. The New Testament has an eschatological outlook; it keeps before us the coming of the Lord as the glorious hope. But it also lays tremendous stress on the stupendous fact of the Incarnation of our Lord and on the decisive significance of His death, resurrection, and ascension. These events were so decisive as to usher in 'the last times' (Heb. 1:2; 9:26; 1 John 2:18; 1 Cor. 10:11), and through them Christ's people are already in possession of eternal life and are even now seated in heavenly places in Him.

In Matthew 28:18–20 we have clear witness to the decisive nature of our Lord's death and resurrection. There He claimed to have been invested with universal authority, gave the great commission to His disciples, and promised His continued presence with them till the consummation. In 1 Corinthians 15, too, we are brought right up to the perfected kingdom of God (e.g., in verses 50–55), but it is strongly emphasised that in the meantime Christ is reigning and abolishing all rule and authority and power, and that He must reign till all His foes are subdued, the last of these being death, which is 'swallowed up in victory' at the resurrection of the saints (verses 24–26, 54).

We may well expect then to find in the Book of Revelation this emphasis which we have in the rest of the New Testament – an emphasis not only on the great climactic end-time event, but on the establishing and preserving of the Church in the meantime and on Christ's continued presence with her. This is just what we do find. The vision of the exalted Christ in chapter 1 strikes the key-note, or at least gives the perspective of the whole book. The Lord is in the midst of the candlesticks and claims to possess the keys of death and hell. The vision of Him is in close connection with the Seven Letters of chapters 2 and 3, but it is also introductory to the whole book. That this is so is plain from the fact that leading items in the description of our Lord in chapter 1 are repeated not only in chapters 2 and 3, but in chapter 19 (verses 12, 15, and 21). The Lord, therefore, is throughout in the midst of His Church and is Head over all things, having the keys of all realms.

In chapter 1 we see Christ's kingdom already present in John's time, for His people can say: 'He has constituted us a kingdom' (v. 6, R.V.). John and his fellow-believers were members of this kingdom (v. 9), and without doubt its future fortunes were a matter of great concern to them. Its very existence was seriously threatened just then – under a persecuting emperor. For their comfort, John sets forth the 'broad sweep' of its eventful story. He is commanded to write of 'things which are now taking place and those which are to follow' (Rev. 1:19, see Weymouth's *New Testament in Modern Speech*) – a description which seems to indicate that the book has to do with the whole history of Christ's kingdom up to the consummation. The book keeps the glorious hope and the grand finale before us, but abounds also in teaching relating to the Christian's present struggle. It calls on him to fight valiantly and comforts him with the thought of redemption already won and with the thought of the conquering Lamb even now in the midst of the throne. In other words, the Book of Revelation insists on the tremendous importance of what

Christ is going to do, but rings the changes also on what He has done and is doing.

If the book is concerned with the whole history of Christ's kingdom, is it history without a break? It seems particularly clear at the end of chapter 11 that it is not. In chapters 10 and 11, under the last of the seven trumpets, it is proclaimed that time shall be no longer and that the mystery of God is finished, His servants rewarded, and the wicked punished. Thereupon, chapter 12 conducts us back to the first advent – the birth of Christ and His Ascension on high. Professor Kromminga, one of the latest advocates of the continuous history view, admits a going back here to the beginning of the Gospel era. In fact, there are so many cases of going back – of recapitulation – and also of antici- pation in the book, and so many isolated episodes, that the continuous history view is clearly erroneous. Indeed, any view which attempts to fit in the details of the book with the panorama of the events of history is unworkable. The very diversity of interpretation among adherents of this school is in itself witness to this. It would indeed fare ill with the poor and unlearned in their study of the book if the view were correct. Few of us are masters of the history of these nineteen centuries. God has, we feel sure, not left the interpretation of the book so altogether dependent on an acquaintance with Church history.

Revelation then presents the great drama of the conflict between Christ and His people on the one hand and Satan and his followers on the other. It covers the unfolding of the entire history of Christ's kingdom from the beginning of the Christian era to the grand climax at the second advent.[1]

---

[1]For a setting forth of this point of view, see William Hendriksen's *More Than Conquerors* (Tyndale Press).

13 : *The witness of Revelation*

IN an examination of the Book of Revelation, some features should particularly be noticed:

The Use of Symbols

The Book is by and large a book of symbols. There is indeed what one may call didactic writing in it. For example, there are plain statements about the second advent. But the attempts to carry through a literal interpretation founder on the rock of the patently symbolic character of much of it. It is written in sign language for the most part. The bulk of it was communicated by visions. John was (literally 'became') in the Spirit on the Lord's day and the unseen world was opened to him and, as in a great drama, successive visions passed before his view. Think of Peter's vision in Acts 10. Being in a trance, Peter saw a great sheet let down by the four corners, wherein were all manner of four-footed beasts and creeping things and birds. Peter, though slow at first, came to see that this vision was full of significance – preparing him to recognise that God was no respecter of persons and that He would freely receive Gentiles who believed, as well as believing Jews. So it is with the visions seen by John. If we take them literally, we are in grave danger of getting only the husk, while missing the kernel – the true meaning. There are those who insist on taking a grossly literal view. The book bears on the very face of it a warning against such treatment. It speaks, for example, of 'a woman sitting on seven mountains', but no female ever had such sitting capacity! It speaks also of a wonder in heaven, a woman in birth-pangs, 'clothed with the sun and the moon under her feet, and upon her head a crown of twelve stars', and goes on to speak of this same woman as having 'the two wings of a great eagle'. Do not the very terms of description warn us against taking these statements literally?

In Revelation 14:4 we read: 'These are they which were not defiled with women; for they are virgins. . . . These were redeemed from among men.' To our consistently literalist friends this must surely be a piece of confusion to unravel!

We read, 'the shapes of the locusts were like unto horses preparing unto battle, and on their heads were as it were crowns like gold, and their faces were as the faces of men, and they had hair as the hair of women, and their teeth as the teeth of lions. And they had breastplates as it were breastplates of iron, and the sound of their wings was as the sound of chariots of many horses running to battle' (Rev. 9:7-10). Again, we read of 'a great hail out of heaven, every stone about the weight of a talent' (more than 100 lb.); and of carnage so great that there is a sea of blood over 200 miles in length, reaching to the horses' bridles (Rev. 16:21; 14:20). To take any of these figures literally is to spoil the impression. The details are given simply to show us the fearsomeness and gruesomeness of the things portrayed.

There are not wanting direct intimations that what John is giving is not literal description, but pictures. In chapter 19:11-21 we have the Saviour coming, King of kings and Lord of lords, on a white horse, with a sword, and the fowls of heaven are summoned to eat the flesh of His foes, whom He shall overthrow. Here we have a vivid picture of a complete victory and all the imagery of war is employed to give it life. But the passage contains a warning, twice repeated, that this is not literal war. Twice over the writer tells us that the implement of victory is a sword which 'proceeded out of the mouth' of the Conqueror. We are not to conceive of the Lord of glory as in hand-to-hand grapple with His foes. He needs but to speak, as He did in Gethsemane (John 18:6), and His enemies fall prostrate.

The great blood-red dragon of chapter 12, John plainly tells us, is the devil. The beasts in chapter 13, somewhat like the beasts in Daniel, set before us anti-Christian powers, political and religious. In a recent booklet *Communism and Christianity*, David Bentley-Taylor says: 'It is a matter for great regret that the Book of Revelation is so little expounded among Christians. . . . Nowhere else in Scripture is the position of the Lord's people in China so vividly and accurately depicted as here. If you want to sense the atmosphere, read the 13th chapter of Revelation and set down Chinese Christians . . . in the midst of it. The first ten verses suggest the force which faces them; the remaining eight verses give an idea of the propaganda and efficiency which are associated with it.' In other words, this is a case of the beast out of the sea and the beast out of the earth before our eyes.

A Progress Towards the Climax

There is a progress in the book towards the great climax. The Seven Letters (chapters 2–3) form a section. The rest of the book falls into six sections. In each of these sections John leads us to the end and then begins again from an earlier point. There is a considerable amount of parallelism betwixt the various sections, and that the book moves with increasing crescendo to the climax may be seen if we look at the finale in each section—

Chapter 6 leads to the near approach of the end, with men crying to the mountains and rocks, Fall on us and hide us from the face of Him that sitteth on the throne, for the great day of His wrath is come.

Chapter 11 again ushers in the end, with the last trump proclaiming that time shall be no more.

Chapter 14 pictures the end under the figure of a two-fold harvest – the ingathering of the wheat and the ingathering of the grapes.

Chapter 16 leads to the voice from the throne, saying, It is done, and to the giving of the cup of the wine of the fierceness of God's wrath.

Chapter 19 leads to the coming of the Conqueror on the white horse, King of kings and Lord of lords, victorious over all His foes.

Chapter 20 brings us to the great white throne, with all the dead, small and great, standing before God, a scene which is followed by the glorious picture of the new heavens and new earth – the absolute consummation.

There is here, without doubt, a progress to a climax.

A Harmony with the Rest of Scripture

In our examination of the teaching of the New Testament on the second advent, we have left the Book of Revelation till now, not merely because it is the last book of the Bible, but because it is a sound principle that precise and clear Scriptures be our guide in interpreting the figurative and more obscure. 'Within due limits,' says B. B. Warfield, 'surely the order of investigation should be from the clearer to the more obscure.'

We have seen that there is no mention whatever of a thousand-year reign of Christ on earth in the rest of the New Testament. Not only does the word 'millennium' not occur elsewhere, but the conception is unknown outside of Revelation 20. Even where Paul is expressly dealing with the Jews and their future, as in Romans 11, he makes no mention of the national restoration and national pre-eminence of the Jews under the sceptre of the Messiah in the millennium, which we would expect him to make, if these things were to be. To take from this passage (Rev. 20), imperfectly understood, the idea of a millennium and forcibly impose it upon the rest of Scripture is the common procedure. Yet, not only is the conception absent from the rest of Scripture, it is also, as we have seen, definitely excluded by the teaching of many passages.

The unanimous testimony of the Gospels, the Acts and the Epistles is that the second advent has as its accompaniments the general resurrection and the final judgment of all. Have we this teaching in the Book of Revelation also? Most certainly.

Revelation 10:7 reads: 'In the days of the voice of the seventh angel, when he shall begin to sound, then is finished the mystery of God.' The next chapter tells us that 'the seventh angel sounded' and the twenty-four elders say, 'Thy wrath is come and the time of the dead, that they should be judged, and that thou shouldest give reward to thy servants the prophets, and to the saints, and them that fear thy name, small and great; and shouldest destroy them that destroy the earth' (Rev. 11:15–18). Here is the end, and at the end the dead are judged, God's saints rewarded, and the wicked destroyed. The Book of Revelation speaks of a general judgment as does the rest of Scripture.

Revelation 16:14–16 is also worth noting. The three unclean spirits 'go forth unto the kings of the whole world, to gather them to the battle of the great day of God Almighty. Behold I come as a thief. Blessed is he that watcheth, and keepeth his garments, lest he walk naked, and they see his shame. And he gathered them together into a place called in the Hebrew tongue Armageddon.' The common school of pre-millenarians (e.g. Charles Feinberg) take Christ's 'coming as a thief' to be at 'the rapture'. Here, however, it is put at what they regard as the close of the time of the great tribulation *after* the rapture!

In Revelation 20:11–15 we read of the great white throne and of the dead, small and great, standing before God. 'And the books were opened; and another book was opened, which is the book of life; and the dead were judged out of those things which were written in the books, according to their works, and death and hell were cast into the lake of fire. This is the second death. And whosoever was not found written in the book of life was cast into the lake of fire.' Dr Warfield comments: 'That this is the *general* judgment seems to be obvious on the face of it. Those whom it concerns are described as "the dead, both small and great", which seems to be an inclusive designation. That it is not merely the wicked who are summoned to it appears from the fact that not only the "book of deeds", but also the "book of life" (twice mentioned) is employed in it, and it is only those whose names are not found written in the book of life that are cast into the lake of fire, whence it seems to follow that some are present whose names are written in the "book of life". The destruction of "death and Hades" does not imply that the judgment is over the enemies of God only, but merely that hereafter, as Paul, too, says (1 Cor. 15), death shall be no more. There is, no doubt, the "second death", but this is the lake of fire, that is to say, the eternal torment. It is, thus, the great final assize that is here presented to our contemplation; implying the general resurrection and preparing the entrance into eternal destiny.'

Thus the Book of Revelation joins in the unanimous testimony to a general resurrection and general judgment.

One well-known passage remains to be examined – the passage which has given rise to the idea of an earthly millennium and which is looked upon as its stronghold, namely, Revelation 20. The Scofield Bible admits that it is this passage which has given rise to the notion.

14: *The pre-millennial view of Revelation 20*

We may take Walter Scott's *Exposition of the Revelation* as giving the common pre-millennial view. He outlines the chapter as follows: 'There are four great actions: first, the binding of Satan in the abyss for a thousand years (verses 1–3); second, the reign with Christ of all the heavenly saints for a thousand years (verses 4–6); third, Satan's last and desperate attempt to regain the mastery of the world, and his utter defeat and final doom (verses 7–10); fourth, the judgment of the wicked dead (verses 11–15)' (p. 395).

The common pre-millennial view is that the thousand years of Revelation 20 is the period of Christ's earthly reign over restored Israel and the subdued Gentile nations; during this period Satan is bound and evil is repressed, while with Christ reign his resurrected and translated saints; in this millennium Old Testament prophecies about the taming of wild animals, and the restoration of the temple and its worship and ritual are fulfilled; at the end of the millennium Satan is let loose for a short time, and goes forth to stir up the nations to rebel against the beneficent rule of Christ and His saints; in this he is successful and leads an innumerable rebel host, but is overthrown, and then meets his final doom in the lake of fire; the judgment of the wicked ensues. This view we must now consider.

Walter Scott emphasises 'the symbolic character of the scene', as far as the binding of Satan is concerned. He says, 'The angel has the key of the abyss and a great chain in his hand. One need scarcely insist upon the symbolic character of the scene, for *that* seems evident on the surface.' Scott points out that the *symbols* of key, chain, and seal signify that 'by angelic agency' Satan's 'liberty is curtailed and his sphere of operations narrowed'. After admitting the use of symbol in verse 1, Scott denies the use of symbol in verses 2 and 4 – the key and the chain are symbols, but not the thousand years. The thousand years, he says, 'in our judgment, should be regarded not in any symbolic sense, but as describing the exact and literal denomination of time. The term *the millennium* as a designation referring to the period of the Lord's reign – public and personal with His saints – over the earth is gathered from this chapter' (p. 398).

It is certainly to the good that Scott admits that as Satan is a spiritual being, the key and chain must carry spiritual significance and are not to be regarded as material objects. We must lodge an emphatic protest, however, at the unjustifiable way in which Scott mingles the symbolic and the literal at his own mere whim. One term is symbol because he chooses to take it so, while another in the next or even in the same verse must be taken in an absolutely literal sense. This feature marks Scott's commentary on Revelation at other points, and marks the entire pre-millennial interpretation.

Those who take the number one thousand as literal pay no regard to the use of numbers in Revelation. The numbers speak a language. Even Walter Scott does not take the number seven as absolutely literal; the seven churches he admits to be 'representative of the Church universal'. But why should one number be symbolic and not another? Bishop Wordsworth calls attention to the fact that the number one thousand is used more than twenty times in Revelation, and adds, '*Not once*, as I believe, is it used *literally*. It is employed as a perfect number.' Professor William Milligan says, 'If we interpret the thousand years literally, it will be a solitary example of a literal use of numbers in the Apocalypse, and this objection alone is fatal.'

How do pre-millenarians get a reign on earth into verses 4–6? There is no indication that it is such. In fact, John is careful to say that he saw 'the *souls* of them that were beheaded'. Here is clear indication that the vision relates, not to glorified saints having their glorified bodies, but to those in the disembodied state in the Paradise of God. Verse 4 reads: 'And I saw thrones, and they sat upon them, and judgment was given unto them: and I saw the souls of them that had been beheaded for the testimony of Jesus and for the word of God, and such as worshipped not the beast, neither his image, and received not the mark upon their forehead and upon their hand; and they lived, and reigned with Christ a thousand years' (R.V.). There is no authority whatever for placing the thrones *on earth*. Let the pre-millenarian, who is so strict in holding us to the letter of the passage as to a literal thousand years, stick to what the passage actually says. Elsewhere in Revelation such thrones are located *in heaven* (Revelation 4:4, where the pre-millenarians themselves take those sitting on the thrones to be the company of the redeemed and glorified *in heaven*).

Another great difficulty for the pre-millenarian, with his insistence on the exact letter, is the identification of those who sit on the thrones. Only two companies are definitely mentioned – those beheaded for the testimony of Jesus and those who refused to submit to the beast. But the pre-millenarians badly want to get in here a resurrection of *all* the righteous. Walter Scott feels this difficulty, and manages to introduce *all* the righteous under the words 'they' and 'them' in the first part of verse 4. He says, 'The "they" evidently refers to a well-known class; . . . they are the sum of Old Testament and New Testament believers, raised or changed at the Coming into the air. This is a much larger body of saints than the martyrs, and hence you have nowhere to locate them in the reign, save as included under the two plural pronouns they and them.' The fact remains that there is *no* mention of *all* the righteous in verse 4 literally interpreted.

Walter Scott takes those beheaded and those who refused to submit to the beast to be those martyred in the tribulation period after the 'rapture' of the saints, and he says that they have a resurrection on the eve of Christ's millennial reign on earth, that is, at the close of the tribulation period and years after the resurrection of the other saints. This he takes from the words, 'the souls of them that had been beheaded for the testimony of Jesus; . . . they lived, and reigned with Christ a thousand years. . . . This is the first resurrection.' As a matter of fact, on Scott's own interpretation, it would not be the *first* resurrection, for the first would have taken place years before at the time of the 'rapture'!

A. R. Fausset, a learned pre-millenarian expositor, admits the difficulty of getting *all* the righteous into verse 4, on the basis of his literal interpretation. He says, 'the *extent* of the first resurrection is not spoken of here', and he refers us for that to 1 Corinthians 15 and 1 Thessalonians 4. Pre-millenarians would sometimes have us believe that their whole millennial scheme lies plain as a pikestaff in Revelation 20; but very evidently it is not so.

The pre-millennial view of an earthly reign of a thousand years involves these paradoxes: (1) The glorified saints will be on an earth which is not 'glorified' or renovated, that is, which has not yet received its cleansing fiery bath; (2) Saints with glorified bodies will mingle with saints and sinners who have not glorified bodies. This would be 'a mixum gatherum'; (3) Satan will be bound so as to deceive the nations no more, yet these nations continue at heart enemies of Christ, ready to obey Satan and to war against the saints the moment the thousand years are finished. They seem even to be more in number than the righteous at the end of the millennium, for *they* are as the sand of the sea, while the righteous are gathered in a beleaguered 'camp' and 'city', and only fire from heaven saves this feeble camp from the assault.

Confronting the literal view taken by the pre-millenarians there are very formidable difficulties arising from the passage itself; there is also the difficulty of reconciling this view with what we have seen to be the unanimous testimony of the rest of the New Testament, in which there is plain and clear instruction given as to the second coming.[1] A much more satisfactory view of Revelation 20 will be presented in the next chapter.

[1]Many Scriptures which are quoted to support the idea of Christ reigning on earth for a thousand years really set forth an *eternal* reign, e.g., 2 Sam. 7:16; Is. 9:7; Dan. 2:44; 7:14; Luke 1:33.

15 : *Satan, a defeated and doomed foe*

Iɴ the Book of Revelation, from chapter 12 on, three great enemies of our Lord and His saints are prominent – Satan the great blood-red dragon, the beast and the false prophet (the second beast of Revelation 13 is in later chapters called the false prophet). In chapter 19 we have the victory of the Word of God, the King of kings and Lord of lords, over His enemies. He comes to smite the nations and He secures their complete overthrow. All the armies of His foes are totally destroyed and 'all the birds are filled with their flesh'. This is a vivid picture of complete victory. Christ makes a full end of the beast and the false prophet and *all* their followers, and treads the winepress of the fierceness and wrath of Almighty God. Beyond question, chapter 19 conducts us right up to the end of the world and the complete victory of Christ. But though chapter 19 conducts us right to the end, one thing it does not do. While it shows us the doom of the prime agents of Satan – the beast and the false prophet and their adherents – it does not show us the doom of the lurking deceiver himself. That is now to be shown us. So the main theme of the first ten verses of Revelation 20 is the *overthrow* of Satan.

In depicting this overthrow it would not be strange if the apostle John were to conduct us back to the beginning of the Christian era. Such a re-tracing of our steps would be quite in keeping with the structure of the Book of Revelation. For example, in chapters 10 and 11, as we have already pointed out, it seems absolutely clear that with the sounding of the final trumpet, the whole purpose of God in human history is complete ('then is finished the mystery of God', 10:7) and the time is come for the dead to be judged (11:18). Yet after this final end, chapter 12 brings us back to the beginning of the Christian era, for in this chapter we have the picture of the dragon waiting to devour the Man-child and of his defeat and frustration – the Man-child is caught up to God and His throne. It is clear that the Man-child is Christ, for He is described (12:5) as destined to rule the nations with a rod of iron (no doubt, from His throne as Mediator and especially on a future day as Judge). Moreover, when the dragon is cast down a great voice proclaims: 'Now is come . . . the kingdom of our God, and *the authority of his Christ*' (12:10). So then it is the birth of Christ and His victory over Satan, consummated by His ascension to heaven, which chapter 12 sets forth.

A return to the beginning of the Christian era would, then, be quite in keeping with the structure of the Book of Revelation. Moreover, if Christ's conquest over Satan is to be set forth, it would indeed seem necessary to go back to the ministry of Christ and to His cross, for it is the unanimous testimony of the New Testament writers that it was through Christ's victory on the cross that Satan was 'cast down'.

Though Revelation 20 is parallel to other sections of the book, conducting us from the beginning of the Christian era to the great consummation at the last Judgment, yet this section has its own distinctive features. The main picture it presents is of a Thousand Year binding of Satan.

Of this Thousand Year victory over Satan there is an earthly aspect and a heavenly aspect.

The Earthly Aspect (Rev. 20:1–3; 7–10)

In verses 1–3 of Revelation 20 the binding of Satan is set forth. Is this binding described in literal or symbolic language? Without doubt there is symbolism here. Even a devoted literalist like Walter Scott admits that the key and the chain and the seal in these verses are symbols. But if they are symbols, may not the Thousand Years for which they are used be a symbol also?

When we speak of the term 'The Thousand Years' as a symbol, it is not implied that there is *no* notion of time in it. It may indicate a long period but that is only a part of its significance. Other instances of the symbolic use of numbers abound in the Book of Revelation. The 'seven spirits' in 1:4 are without doubt the perfect Spirit of God. Who can doubt that the number 666 in 13:18 speaks a language? And as to the city foursquare with its breadth and length and height 12,000 furlongs, if we seek merely to measure out these enormous dimensions, we shall miss the deep meaning. So with the number 1000 – it is the sacred number three added to the sacred number seven to form ten, the number of completeness, and then cubed or raised to the third power. It speaks of the completeness and perfection of Christ's victory over Satan.

Over fifteen hundred years ago Augustine pointed out that this binding of Satan is the same as that referred to by our Lord when He spoke of 'binding the strong man' (Matt. 12:26–29). The strong man is Satan, and Christ is the stronger than he who has come to bind him and spoil his goods. Christ is referring to what He came into this world to do. Isaiah 53, which speaks of the sufferings of

Christ, speaks also of the fruits of those sufferings – 'He shall divide the spoil with the strong.' Through His sufferings He was to conquer Satan, and He would not fail to secure the spoils of the conquest.

Many find great difficulty in conceiving of Satan as now 'bound', in view of all the darkness and false religion and devilishness prevailing among the nations of the earth. They should note, first of all, that equally strong language is used of Satan's present condition in plain portions of Scripture. Paul describes Christ as despoiling and triumphing over Satan and his hosts by the cross (Col. 2:15), and the writer of Hebrews speaks of Christ as 'bringing him to nought' by His death (2:14). Jesus Himself just before He went to the cross said that Satan was now to be cast out and judged (John 12:31; 16:11). Indeed the victory was so sure that He speaks of it as already won.

Robert Strong tells us that in the early part of 1938 *The Sunday School Times*, a strongly pre-millennial weekly paper, presented a cartoon by E. J. Pace, which most interestingly and vividly set forth the New Testament conception of a bound and frustrated Satan. This is his description of the cartoon: 'In the background stands the cross of Calvary. In the foreground crouches Satan, labelled also "The Strong Man of Matthew 12:29". He is bound with chains and looks forebodingly over his left shoulder to the dreadful place of "everlasting fire, prepared for the devil and his angels". The cartoon is headed "A Defeated and Doomed Foe" and beneath the heading appeared the interpretative verses: "The Son of God was manifested, that he might destroy the works of the devil" (1 John 3:8); ". . . that through death he might bring to nought him that had the power of death, that is, the devil"

(Heb. 2:14, R.V.).' Dr Strong suggests that all the cartoon needs to make it complete as a striking pictorial representation of the New Testament teaching as to the 'binding' of Satan is the single added line 'Note also Revelation 20:2'. It is surely worthy of remark that the Scofield Bible Notes speak of Satan as 'permitted a certain power' in this Gospel age and add that this is only 'a strictly permissive and limited power'.

It should be noted, secondly, that this conquest over Satan is consistent with a continuing restless activity on his part which is permitted him by God. In the Gospels, when the disciples returned from a mission marked, among other features, by the expulsion of demons, Jesus said, 'I beheld Satan *fallen* as lightning from heaven.' Yet this 'fall' did not incapacitate Satan from all activity – he put forth the utmost of his power against Christ not long after. In 2 Peter 2:4 we read: 'God spared not the angels that sinned, but cast them down to hell, and delivered them into chains of darkness, to be reserved unto judgment.' Chief among the angels that sinned was Satan, and he is here described as 'cast down' and 'delivered into chains'. Yet the same Peter says: 'Your adversary the devil, as a roaring lion, walketh about, seeking whom he may devour' (1 Peter 5:8). It is quite clear from these passages that Satan's 'fall' and his 'chains' are quite consistent with his continuing restless activity among men. So also the 'binding' of Satan in Revelation 20 does not mean the complete cessation of his activities. His case might be compared in some respects to that of Al Capone, the captured gangster, of whom it was said (with exaggeration, no doubt) that he ruled Chicago from Chicago jail. Satan is indeed bound, but he has been given a long chain!

It should be noted, thirdly, that this passage (Rev. 20) speaks of a *particular* restraint that is put upon Satan. Again and again in the Scriptures Satan is shown to be under restraint. In the first two chapters of Job Satan is very active, yet he is under restraint. He is permitted to smite Job's property, but not his body. When this restriction is waived, he is still under restraint, for he is prohibited from taking his life – in this respect he is bound. The Book of Revelation too as a whole presents Satan as active, yet under a curb. In chapter 9, when evil forces are let loose, the key of the pit of the abyss has to be used for their release. The one who uses it is 'a star fallen from heaven', that is, Satan; but note that he does not have the right to the key – it is *given* him. Moreover, in chapter 12 he makes war against the woman and her seed, but is completely unsuccessful. He would seem to be in a position to sweep all before him; but there is a divine hand baffling his efforts. In other words, he is under restraint.

In Revelation 20 it is stated that Satan is bound 'that he should deceive the nations no more, till the thousand years should be fulfilled' (verse 3, cp. verse 8). The particular purpose of the binding that is here stressed is this – he is bound so as 'not to deceive the nations'. It is not stated that the nations will be saved; and if they are not saved, in a very real sense they are still under 'deception'. It seems then that the phrase 'deceive the nations no more' refers to a particular kind of deception not to be exercised by Satan. William Hendriksen refers to the Old Testament times when God suffered the nations to walk in their own ways (Acts 14:16) and he contrasts the widespread knowledge of Christ today. He concludes that 'the binding of Satan and the fact that he is hurled into the abyss to remain there for a thousand years indicates that throughout the present Gospel Age, which begins with Christ's first coming and extends to the second coming, the devil's influence on earth is curtailed so that he is unable to prevent the extension of the church among the nations by means of an active missionary programme.' True though this suggestion may be, the context points to another explanation of the 'deception' which Satan is restrained from exercising. Verse 3 states that the devil will deceive the nations no more, until the thousand years are finished. Verse 7 repeats this thought, and verse 8 adds that he shall then come forth (after the expiry of the thousand years) to deceive the nations, to gather them together to 'the war'. In other words, the 'deception', from which he is now restrained and which he is at the end permitted to exercise, is distinctly stated – he is restrained from 'gathering the nations together to the war' (Greek, 'ton polemon'). Satan is given much scope, but this restriction is put upon him.

What 'the war' is appears from Revelation 16:14–16 and 19:19, where the same great climactic battle is described. It is the battle or the war of the great day of God Almighty. The hour for it has at length come and Satan is allowed to exercise this deception, which he will do on a grand scale for the final worldwide conflict. He will inspire a mass attack upon the church of Christ. The nations whom he will gather are referred to as 'Gog and Magog', terms taken from Ezekiel's description of the enemies of God's people. The three chapters 16, 19, and 20 all speak of this 'gathering together' and of 'the war'. John is picturing the final world-wide oppression of the church of Christ preceding the second Advent. The church might seem on the point of being overwhelmed, but quick as lightning Christ will intervene and discomfit utterly all His and her foes. Then will follow the resurrection and final judgment of all, from the highest ruler to the meanest slave (Rev. 20:11–15).

The Heavenly Aspect (Rev. 20:4–6)

These verses set forth the heavenly aspect of the Thousand Years. Verse 3 speaks of Satan being bound for a Thousand Years, and adds, 'after this he must be loosed for a little while'. Verse 7 repeats the same thought: 'when the thousand years are finished, Satan shall be loosed from his prison, and shall come forth to deceive the nations'. It is clear that verses 7–10 are a direct continuation from verses 1–3, so that the intervening verses 4–6 are in the nature of a parenthesis. This parenthesis speaks of the Thousand Year reign of the saints. Dr Hendriksen asks with regard to this reign the following questions:

1. *Where does this reign take place?*

It should be noted that there is no mention of Palestine or Jerusalem in these verses. The saints are described as seated on thrones (v. 4). As pointed out in the preceding chapter, wherever thrones are mentioned in this book, whether the thrones of Christ or His people, they are located in heaven. The likelihood then is that this is the case here too. That it is indeed so is made plain by the expression, 'I saw the *souls* of them that had been beheaded' (verse 4). 'Souls' are here almost contrasted with 'bodies', for undoubtedly the chapter is not without an emphasis on the bodily resurrection. It is then a vision of disembodied spirits that we have here. The warfare of the saints on earth, which is much to the fore in this book, is only one part of their story on this side of the great final day. The church gathering at home in heaven is the other glorious part.

2. *What is its character?*

Those having part in it are described as 'risen', for they have experienced 'the first resurrection'. Christ's people are in the New Testament declared to be 'risen with Christ' (Col. 3:1; Eph. 2:6; Rom. 6:5–8). Their warfare on this earth has been abundantly set forth in this Book, often under symbols; and the bliss of the eternal state after the final resurrection is set forth in chapters 21–22, much of it under symbols also. May we not expect to have some mention of the bliss of the blessed dead which they enjoy before the final resurrection? And if symbolic language is used to set it forth, need we be surprised?

The saints of 'the first resurrection' are set in contrast with 'the rest of the dead' who live not till the Thousand Years are finished. The saints who have gone to heaven are dead as far as the body is concerned, but they live and reign with Christ in glory. 'The rest of the dead' are dead in every sense, bodily and spiritually dead, and they will come to life again (in the body) only to die the dreadful second death. This is the only resurrection they will have. It may be objected that this involves taking the word 'live' in these verses in two different senses – in verse 4 of a spiritual resurrection and in verse 5 of a bodily resurrection. But John elsewhere refers to the same two different kinds of 'life' within a few verses (John 5:25, 28, 29). And in this very passage he uses the word 'death' in two different senses – of bodily and spiritual death (verses 5 and 6). So it is not only permissible to take 'life' here in two different senses; it is almost demanded of us that we so take it.

'They lived and reigned with Christ' (Rev. 20:4). If anyone argues that 'lived' is in the aorist tense (Greek: 'ezēsan') and therefore indicates an event and not a state, we reply that 'reigned' is also an aorist tense and admittedly indicates a state. (Even in Rev. 2:8 where 'ezēsan' is used of the resurrection of Christ, when we place it against its proper background of Rev. 1:18, it evidently refers to a state and means 'He was in a state of death and *became alive for ever*').

What is depicted in this 'reign' of the saints is the bliss of the blessed dead. Their souls are made perfect in holiness, and received into the highest heavens where they behold the face of God in light and glory. 'Blessed are the dead which die in the Lord.'

3. *Who participate in it?*

'I saw thrones, and they sat upon them, and judgment was given unto them: and I saw the souls of them that were beheaded for the witness of Jesus and for the word of God, and which had not worshipped the beast, neither his image, neither had received his mark upon their foreheads, or in their hands: and they lived and reigned with Christ a thousand years.' Beside the indefinite terms 'they' and 'them', there are two expressions used to describe those who live and reign with Christ. They are (*a*) the martyrs, and (*b*) those who have refused 'the mark of earthliness'. Some make two or three groups out of these descriptive terms. It is better to take them of one group, that is, as simply descriptive of faithful Christians in the warfare of the ages. They are His loyal witnesses who have not loved their lives unto the death. They know in their experience the truth of the words, 'No cross, no crown.' This vision depicts them as enjoying their reward in heaven. Christ was exalted after His death to reign as Messianic King at God's right hand. Here his faithful saints are also described as enthroned. To them He grants to sit with Him on His throne, even as He also overcame and sat down with His Father on His throne (Rev. 3:21).

The Thousand Year reign, then, is the long period between the first and second advents of our Lord. Not only does the number 1000 convey the idea of a long period, but also and more particularly it symbolises heavenly completeness, security and blessedness. When he uses the number 1000 to describe it, he has said 'all he could say to convey to our minds the idea of absolute completeness' (B. B. Warfield).

How little of the usual portrayal of the millennium is actually to be found in Revelation 20! Many will answer that the picture can be filled in from the Old Testament prophecies of a 'golden age' on earth; but it seems much better to take these prophecies as fulfilled in the new and transformed universe. After all, the Old Testament prophecies look not for a temporary but for an eternal kingdom.

The interpretation we have presented (of Rev. 20) is absolutely in harmony with the rest of the New Testament which leaves no room for an intermediate kingdom betwixt Christ's present kingdom and the eternal kingdom of glory. It is also in harmony with the pictorial and symbolic nature of much of the contents of the Book of Revelation, and it does full justice to the passage itself.

We have come to the close of our studies of the Scriptures relating to the second advent. We may now conclude by using Robert Strong's summary (with slight alterations):

i. The Gospel age will run on to the second advent, with the Church of Christ continuing its work of gathering together a people for the name of the Lord.

ii. Towards the end of the age an apostasy from the truth will set in, greatly advanced by 'the man of sin', the personal antichrist, who will lead in the great final rebellion against God and His Christ. This will be a time of great testing for God's faithful people.

iii. The Lord Jesus will come visibly and gloriously. He will raise the sainted dead, transform the living believers, and gather all the redeemed to be with Him; He will destroy the antichrist and judge the world; and He will refashion the earth and the heavens to be the abode of everlasting righteousness.

These events attending His coming will be practically simultaneous, so that there will be one great climactic event at the end of the world. He will come *for* His saints – the blessed dead and the living believers – and they shall meet Him in the air. He will then come *with* His saints – the whole company of them in their glorified bodies – and introduce them into the consummate bliss of the new heavens and new earth.

> *I know not, O I know not,*
> *What joys await us there;*
> *What radiancy of glory,*
> *What bliss beyond compare!*

16: *Is the momentous event near?*

WHEN Christ was on earth, some thought the kingdom would come immediately in its glory, but He corrected that notion (Luke 19:11–27). It is true that the exalted Saviour said, 'I come quickly' (Rev. 22:20), but we must remember that from the divine standpoint the advent is always near, for to Him a thousand years are as one day (2 Peter 3:8), and also that the New Testament conceives of this whole age as 'the last days' (Heb. 1:1, 2; 1 John 2:18).

Are there any indications given in the Scriptures to forewarn of His glorious appearing? Certain events are mentioned, of which these are the chief:

The Calling of the Gentiles

The ministry of pastors and teachers is to continue until all the elect are gathered in and the whole Church is brought to the stature of perfection in Christ (Eph. 4:11–13). All nations are to hear the Gospel through the instrumentality of Christ's servants, and then the end shall come (Matt. 29:19, 20; 24:14). This does not mean that every individual must hear, much less be saved. It means that the nations as a whole will have opportunity given them and that there will be those out of every nation among the redeemed (Rev. 7:9).

The Conversion of Israel

Charles Hodge insists that Romans 11 teaches a national conversion of the Jews to God. G. Vos agrees that 'in the future there will be a comprehensive conversion of Israel'. Some expositors have taken 'all Israel' in Romans 11:26 to denote the spiritual Israel, while Louis Berkhof and William Hendriksen take it as meaning 'the whole number of the elect out of the ancient covenant people'. We agree with Bishop Waldegrave's careful statement: 'It is likely,' he says on Romans 11, 'that a very general turning of Israel to the Lord' shall precede the advent. See John Murray's exposition of this chapter in his *Epistle to the Romans*, New International Commentary Series.

This does not mean that every individual Israelite shall be saved but that conversions will take place among them on a scale unknown before. Our Lord said towards the close of His ministry on earth that the Jews would not see Him till they would hail Him as blessed; in other words, the attitude of a great body of Jews at His second advent would be a changed attitude (Matt. 23:39; Luke 13:15). Let no one say that this puts the advent far into the future. Just as God has made light to travel at the terrific speed of 186,000 miles in one second, so He can when He pleases send forth the light of His Gospel and speedily bring in the full number of His elect from Gentiles and Jews.

We are concerned to point out – against much present-day dispensationalist teaching – that blessing will come to the Jews only in one way, namely, through faith in Christ (Rom. 11:23); that salvation will come to them only through the Gospel of sovereign grace (Rom. 11:32; Acts 4:12); and that there is no hope for a Jew simply as a Jew. He must, like the Gentile sinner, repent and be converted that his sins may be blotted out (Acts 3:19). There is no distinction between Jew and Greek (Rom. 10:12); they must alike be saved by the atoning Saviour. To hold forth hope for the Jew simply as a Jew, as some dispensationalists do, is to preach another Gospel (Gal. 1:8).

Is it proper to hail the return of unconverted, rebellious Jews to Palestine as a fulfilment of prophecy? It would not seem to be so, for prophecy closely links the ideas of conversion and 'restoration' (see Deut. 30:8–10; Ezek. 20:38). Old Testament promises of restoration to the land had a partial fulfilment in the return from the captivity in Babylon. They reach their complete fulfilment in the coming of the spiritual Israel, Abraham's innumerable seed (Gal. 3:29; Rom. 4:16–18), to their true home in Christ and at length to their inheritance in the new heavens and new earth (2 Pet. 3:13; Rev. 21:1). Believing Jews and Gentiles are the true circumcision (Phil. 3:3), citizens of the heavenly Jerusalem (Gal. 4:26), and comers to Mount Zion (Heb. 12:22). We have already shown in chapter 6 that the New Testament gives an enlarged meaning and a spiritual significance to Old Testament promises in which, at first sight, the Jew might seem to be exclusively interested.

The Coming of Antichrist

The anti-Christian principle was at work in the times of the apostles (2 Thess. 2:7; 1 John 2:18). It will reach its highest power just before the advent, there will be a great apostasy, and the anti-Christian power will most likely be concentrated in one individual, the embodiment of all wickedness (2 Thess. 2).

The question is often asked – Will the world become

better or worse towards the coming of the Lord? There are passages in the Bible which seem to teach very clearly that the world at His coming will be a very wicked place like the world of Noah's day or of Lot's day (e.g. Matt. 24:37-42). And there are other passages which seem to set forth a gradual development of Christ's kingdom (e.g., Matt. 13:31-33). Both pictures are, no doubt, true. As R. B. Kuiper says: 'Broadly speaking, conditions on earth are becoming better and worse at once. Witness the Christianization of pagan nations and the slipping back of Christian people into paganism.' It is likely that 'as the reign of the truth will be gradually extended, so the power of evil will gather force towards the end' (G. Vos).

While the above events are clearly set forth as antecedent to the Coming, no one but God knows the time of its occurrence. It will take people by surprise. None of the signs given is of such a nature as to make clear 'the day and hour'. Moreover, let us remember that Christ's first coming was heralded by signs, yet it took all, or nearly all, by surprise – the majority paid little or no attention to them.

Augustine said, 'That day lies hid, that every day we may be on the watch.' Dissenting from the dogmatism of some in his day who held the coming to be imminent, he said very beautifully, 'He who loves the coming of the Lord is not he who affirms that it is far off, nor is it he who says that it is near; but rather he who, whether it be far off or near, awaits it with sincere faith, steadfast hope, and fervent love.'

Epilogue

Dionysius of Alexandria, surnamed 'the Great', was born about A.D. 190, and died in 265. Brought up to a secular profession, with bright prospects of wealth and fame, he was won over to the Christian faith, and could then say, 'What things were gain to me, those I counted loss for Christ.' Eusebius, in his *Ecclesiastical History*, tells us of two works by Dionysius on 'the Promises'. They were written to counteract the teaching of Nepos, a bishop in Egypt, who taught that the promises should be understood more as the Jews understood them. Nepos 'supposed that there would be a certain millennium of sensual luxury on this earth.' To establish his opinion, he wrote a work on the Revelation of John. This was warmly opposed by Dionysius in his two works on the Promises. In the second of these he makes mention of Nepos, now deceased, and of the great stress which his followers laid on his work on Revelation, in which he taught a future earthly reign of Christ. Dionysius speaks of his great love and esteem for Nepos, on account of his faith and industry, his study of the Scriptures, his great attention to psalmody, and the manner in which he departed this life. But, says Dionysius, the truth is to be honoured and loved before all. So he felt bound to write in opposition to the views of Nepos. He states that at Arsinoe, where this doctrine of Nepos prevailed, it led to 'schisms and apostacies of whole churches'.

Dionysius tells us that he visited Arsinoe, and 'after I had called the presbyters and teachers of the brethren in the villages, when those brethren had come who wished to be present, I exhorted them to examine the doctrine publicly. When they had produced this book (of Nepos on Revelation) as a kind of armour and impregnable fortress, I sat with them for three days, from morning till evening, attempting to refute what it contained'. Dionysius pays tribute to the intelligent and teachable spirit of these brethren, and shows in how wise and conciliatory a manner he carried on the discussion with them, not attempting to evade objections and endeavouring, as far as possible, to keep to the subject. The supreme aim was that truth might prevail, and that they should receive whatever was established by the proofs and doctrines of the Holy Scriptures. At length, the founder and leader of the doctrine, Coracio, in the hearing of all the brethren present, 'confessed and avowed to us', that he would no longer adhere to it, as he had been fully convinced by the opposite arguments. In this the other brethren present rejoiced.

If we have failed to be as tactful and conciliatory as Dionysius in presenting our case, we are sincerely sorry. But we do trust that many of our beloved brethren in the Lord, who differ from us on the matters under discussion in this book, will consider their position again. They have perhaps all along heard speakers harp on an earthly reign for a thousand years centred at Jerusalem, and what they have read has been on the same lines; but now they have before them another view, which we believe to be the Scriptural view and the view of the Reformers and Puritans. May it win the allegiance of our readers!

Appendix: The seventy weeks of Daniel 9

D<small>ANIEL</small>'S seventy weeks (or seventy 'sevens') are the basis of many charts of the ages. It is well to note the purpose for which the seventy weeks are decreed: 'Seventy weeks are decreed upon thy people and upon the holy city, to finish transgression, and to make an end of sins, and to make reconciliation for iniquity, and to bring in everlasting righteousness, and to seal up vision and prophecy, and to anoint the most holy' (Dan. 9:24).

These six results mentioned are, according to Daniel, to be fulfilled *before* the expiry of the seventy weeks. It is wrong then to take them (or some of them) as fulfilled in a millennium *after* the seventy weeks, as is commonly done. The bringing of sin to an end and the reconciliation for iniquity took place through Him who 'appeared to put away sin by the sacrifice of Himself' (Heb. 9:26). He brought in a righteousness which endures for ever (2 Cor. 5:21); after His ministry and that of His apostles no prophetic revelation would be needed; and He was the most Holy One anointed with the Spirit (Acts 10:38). Christ is the outstanding figure in the passage. It is said of Him in verse 26 that 'He shall have nothing' or be despised and rejected (see margin of A.V.), and it is He Who 'confirms' or 'causes to prevail' (not 'makes') the covenant, that is, the covenant of grace, which is from of old (v. 27). The one who makes desolate (v. 27b) is Titus, the Roman commander, whose dread ravages are described by Josephus. The procedure of those who separate the 70th week from the 69th, by an interval already far greater than the whole of the 70 weeks, is altogether unjustified. If someone answers that Daniel himself makes a break, it should be pointed out in reply that he makes two (7 weeks and 62 weeks and 1 week). Every interpreter takes the 62 weeks as following the first 7 weeks without interval; the sequence of time is not interrupted; the break simply marks a great event in Israel's history – the restoration of Jerusalem under Ezra and Nehemiah. Similarly, there is no interval between the 69th and 70th weeks – the break simply marks the eventful appearance of Christ. (We are not justified in taking the 70 'sevens' as 490 years. Nowhere in the Old Testament is a period of seven years called a week or 'a seven'. It is best with Keil to take these 'sevens' as 'an intentionally indefinite designation of a period of time, measured by the number 7, whose chronological duration must be determined on other grounds'.)